Pacific Market-places

A collection of essays

Edited by

H. C. BROOKFIELD

AUSTRALIAN NATIONAL UNIVERSITY PRESS

Canberra 1969

First published 1969

Printed and manufactured in Australia

Registered in Australia for transmission by post as a book

Library of Congress Catalog Card no. 69-15736
National Library of Australia reg. no. AUS 68-988
SBN 7081 0040 6

Preface

This volume had its origin in a suggestion by E. K. Fisk. Early in 1967 it was found that five studies of markets in the Pacific area had been prepared for publication about the same time, four of them within the Australian National University. It was felt that these would have greater utility if published side by side in a single volume, permitting comparison between markets, than if presented as separate papers. In two editorial essays I have tried to widen the comparison further, and to discuss some of the problems of interpretation that arise.

These market studies are not truly parallel, except that all of them arose as by-products of other research. The data on which they are based are somewhat unequal, most obviously in the length of time that the markets were kept under observation. These periods range from only a single market day at Apia, supplemented by casual observation as buyer over a longer period, to regular data collection over five months at Honiara. Some of the studies were conducted with a staff of field assistants, others with only one or two assistants; none was carried out by the field worker unaided. The survey methods have much in common: recording of the produce brought to market, prices asked, sales, quantities unsold, accompanied by rather more spasmodic data-gathering among and about the buyers. More than one writer reports weaknesses and problems in his own data. Some writers attempt to relate price to weight, or even to calorific value; others follow market practice in concentrating on value, largely or wholly disregarding weight. Possibly the most efficiently collected and presented data are those derived from the single survey at Apia; certainly the most comprehensive are those presented for Honiara, and the discussion of Honiara market is also distinguished by a depth of understanding not approached in the other studies.

The experiments in survey method may prove of some interest to other workers, but perhaps the principal methodological lesson to be drawn from this group of essays concerns the advantages derived from linking studies of the market-place with inquiries in the market area. The more this is done, the more adequate is the interpretation. It is because this aspect emerges so strongly from the substantive essays that an attempt is made to develop it further in the introductory and concluding discussions.

All papers have been modified somewhat in the interests of comparability, but authors' style has been interfered with as little as possible. The maps were all drawn, and some reconstructed, by Ian Heyward. The bibliography of all contributions is collected together at the end. Currencies presented a problem, and it was decided initially to convert all into Australian dollars; an exception was made, however, in the case of Western Samoa because this would result in prices being represented in odd numbers of cents, thus giving an unreal picture of marketing practice. Conversions were all made at the rates operating during the period of survey; subsequent changes following British devaluation in November 1967 are disregarded. Australian dollar currency is used in Papua-New Guinea, the Solomons and New Hebrides; Samoan currency was until 1967 at par with the New Zealand pound (later dollar); Fijian currency was at the rate of £1 Fijian to $2.25 Australian from 1940 to 1967; French Pacific francs in New Caledonia and Tahiti have varied around $0.98 to $1.00 Australian; French Pacific francs in the New Hebrides have been pegged at exactly one dollar Australian for some years. All references to dollars mean Australian dollars, which were at the time of survey and are still in 1969 worth approximately $1.12 in United States currency. In the period to which this book refers, they were worth approximately 8s sterling.

A number of people have contributed helpful advice and comment. Paula Glick has commented on the Introduction, and E. K. Fisk and Scarlett Epstein have commented on several parts of the manuscript; the debt of all authors to Mrs Epstein for her pioneer study of Rabaul market (Epstein 1961) emerges repeatedly in the text. Two anonymous referees have made a number of most helpful suggestions. Gratitude is also due to a group of tolerant authors, who cheerfully endured my tinkering with their manuscripts. The editorial staff of the A.N.U. Press has pointed to a large number of minor deficiencies, and has smoothed some infelicities of style. I am grateful to Mrs B. M. Banks for undertaking the onerous task of preparing the index. Above all, however, I would thank my research assistant, Mrs Doreen Hart. In addition to being part-author of one chapter, she has done a great deal of work on the whole volume and has made a great number of major and minor comments and criticisms, some of a quite fundamental order. It is not too much to say that the book could hardly have been completed in the time without her. It need scarcely be added that the editor bears prime responsibility for the deficiencies that remain.

Canberra
1969

H. C. Brookfield

Notes on Contributors

R. B. Dakeyne was for some years Senior Tutor in the Department of Geography, University of Sydney. He worked among the Yega people of the Northern District of Papua, with some aid from the Australian National University, and his contribution here is one product of his research. He is at present with the Department of Advisory Services, University of Sydney.

G. R. Hogbin worked for several years as a Research Assistant in the Department of Economics, Australian National University, spending most of this time in New Guinea, where he carried out a range of field surveys. He is now studying at the East-West Center, Honolulu.

I. Q. Lasaqa was trained in Fiji and New Zealand, and in 1968 completed a Ph.D. thesis in Geography at the Australian National University on post-war economic development among Melanesians in northern Guadalcanal. In mid-1968 he returned to Fiji to a post with the University of the South Pacific, Suva.

B. A. Lockwood has completed a Ph.D. thesis in Economics at the Australian National University on market participation and monetisation in Western Samoa; he is a Research Fellow in Economics at this University.

Paula Brown Glick worked for several years in the Department of Anthropology and Sociology at the Australian National University and is the author of numerous papers on the Chimbu of New Guinea, and other topics in the Pacific and North America. She is now Professor of Anthropology at the State University of New York at Stony Brook.

Doreen Hart has been a Research Assistant in the Department of Geography, Australian National University, for some years, where she has worked on several aspects of research in Melanesia.

H. C. Brookfield is a Professorial Fellow in Geography at the Australian National University. He has worked in southern and eastern Africa, Mauritius, New Guinea, and eastern Melanesia. Currently he is preparing a comparative geographical study of the six Melanesian territories.

Contents

Maps

Tables

I

Introduction: The Market-place

H. C. Brookfield

All the market-places discussed in this volume are recently developed, existing to supply urban populations with fresh produce. The goods offered consist mainly of native staple foods, fresh fruit and vegetables, limited quantities of fish, meat, cooked foods, native stimulants, and relishes. There is little trading in local manufactures or export crops. Imported produce hardly appears in the market-places at all now, though historically 'trade goods' such as knives, axes, salt, and tobacco were used to buy local produce. The market-places exist alongside permanently established trade stores, shops, and department stores, operated for the most part by expatriates and companies; these shops handle some local produce, but it is only a minor part of their stock in trade. The market-places discussed here are thus as a whole dissimilar to those of Africa, Asia, or the Caribbean, in which large quantities of imported goods are handled (Belshaw 1965: 53-83; Bohannan and Dalton 1962; Dewey 1962; Bauer 1954: 22-34). Most of them are also much simpler in organisation, being dominated by indigenous producer-sellers who each bring their own produce to market and remain with it until it is sold, or until the market is over. Middlemen and *colporteurs*[1] have emerged on a large scale only in New Caledonia,

[1]The French term *colporteur*, meaning a hawker or a person who buys goods in one place and sells them in another, is here employed to distinguish the middlemen who travel between producing area and market from those middlemen who operate only within the market, buying from producers and selling to customers. There are also some men who act as 'agent middlemen', selling on commission, and others who are in the strict sense hawkers, here restricted to those selling around the town and not in the market-place.

Tahiti, and Fiji, where we do have something like the chain of intermediaries described by Bauer (1954: 22) for West Africa, and where the same intermediary may operate at different times in different market-places. Elsewhere in the Pacific even quite large markets, such as those of Apia, Rabaul, and Honiara, operate almost entirely without such intermediate sellers. There are other distinctive features; overt competition between sellers is largely absent, though prices – or rather quantities offered for the same price – may vary somewhat between different parts of a market-place; nearly all trading is done in silver currency, and there is only rarely any bargaining or haggling except where intermediaries are active. Prices vary in the long term in all markets, and variations between markets do reflect the relative scarcities of produce in relation to demand; however, there is little short-term flexibility in response to daily or hourly variations in supply and demand, even if much produce seems likely to remain unsold. 'Trading partnerships' between buyer and seller – the *pratique* described by Mintz (1959) in Haiti – seem limited in the main to arrangements between producer and middleman or *colporteur*, though in several markets regular customers do receive some advantage from sellers that they know. Participation in the economy of the market-place by surrounding rural populations is very variable, and some Pacific markets draw supplies from a surprisingly wide area. Most of these characteristics were first noted by Epstein (1961) in her pioneer study of Rabaul market in New Britain, and it has since become evident that they are widespread phenomena.

The plan of the book

The five substantive essays here presented describe markets of widely different type within the general framework. Popondetta and Kerema have small, relatively new market-places serving a small urban population, and there are some interesting differences between them. Honiara market, like the first two, is almost wholly dominated by Melanesians, but these include an important group of migrant islanders whose practices contrast with those of the local villagers. Further, there is some significant participation by Asians as carriers to the market, though not as traders or *colporteurs*. This market has grown very rapidly in recent years. Apia market-place is hardly a single site at all: it spills all over the central part of the capital of Western Samoa, giving unusual scope for internal differentiation. A significant proportion of the sellers are part-Samoans, mainly Chinese-Samoans, whose practices are – as with the Malaitans at Honiara – somewhat different from those of the Samoan sellers. In a society where interrelationship is more extensively reckoned than is normal in Melanesia, the market-place is the one place

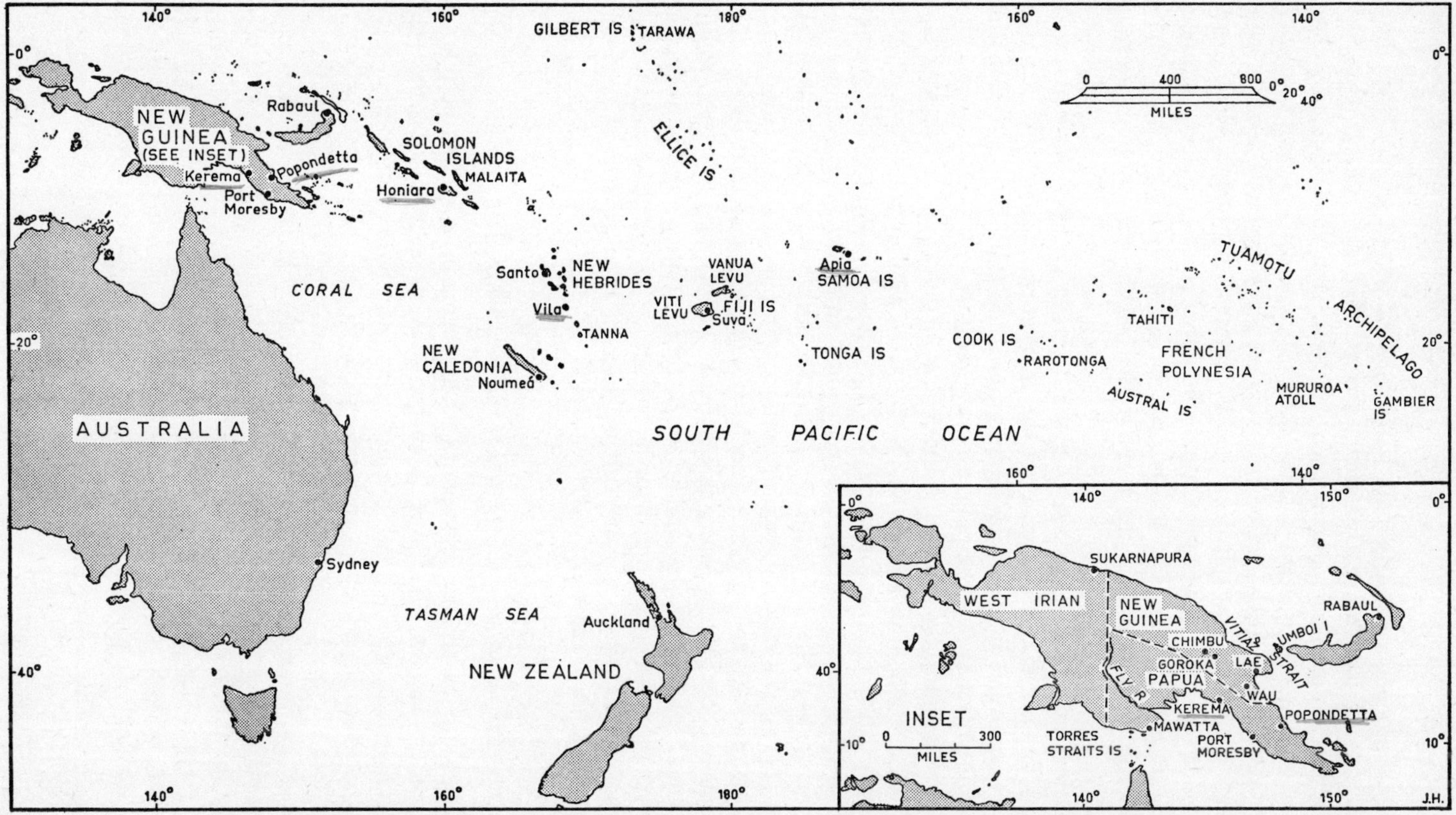

Map 1 *South Pacific Ocean, showing principal islands, territories, and towns mentioned in the text*

where Samoans regularly and habitually exchange goods with other Samoans against money. Lastly, the market at Vila in the New Hebrides is dominated numerically by New Hebridean village sellers, but commercially by a small core-group of specialised market gardeners and middlemen. Ethnically, this market-place is more diverse than others reviewed, since it includes Vietnamese, Chinese, Métis,[2] and European sellers. But more than the other market-places here discussed, that of Vila is overshadowed by company and private shops, and competition between the two for the buyers' money emerges most clearly.

Before and after these five essays are placed two general essays: the first – the present one – concerns the market-place itself, its historical antecedents and modern development, and the trading practices within it. The object is to attempt some interpretation of the trading practices of Pacific markets, especially those dominated by indigenous sellers, and to this end much historical material is introduced to demonstrate possible links between modern and traditional practice. As Belshaw (1965: 76) notes, 'market place systems do not exist in isolation but are flanked on the one hand by prestation and subsistence, and on the other by a fully modern sector'; both flanking sectors affect the nature of the market, and my purpose is to analyse these influences. The second and concluding essay is concerned mainly with the problems of the market area, its size and internal differentiation, and the relationship of this observed pattern to theories of agricultural location around towns. Finally, there is some further attempt to put the Pacific market-place in a theoretical context.

Antecedents: some characteristics of indigenous trade

Social relations are the framework of all forms of economic activity in the Pacific islands. Reciprocal prestation is structured by social relationships and provides the means by which interpersonal ties of all sorts are recognised and maintained, both within and between the local and descent groups into which populations are divided. Valuables of various kinds are often the central commodity in the prestations, but these are generally supplemented by large quantities of foodstuffs, both 'special' foods which are in short supply and are produced mainly for reciprocal giving, and also staple foods required to feed the visitors, helpers, or recipients.[3] This production may attain such proportions that, in the major pig ceremonies of the New Guinea highlands, more

[2]Métis are mixed-bloods of various origins, but mainly either European/Melanesian or Eurasian.

[3]Reciprocity, defined by Polanyi (1957:250) as denoting 'movements between correlative points of symmetrical groupings', now has an extensive theoretical literature, among which particular mention might be made of Belshaw (1965:

than half the total productive resources of a community may be devoted to it. The prestations may include some interregional trade; valuables and 'special' foods may move from areas in which they are plentiful to those in which they are scarce.

Within and above these institutionalised exchanges there are, especially in the New Guinea-Solomons area, much more extensive and formalised patterns of trading, having the form of integrated trading systems over quite wide areas. There is an extensive, if scattered, literature on these systems, on the eastern Papuan systems of Mailu and the Kula Ring (Malinowski 1915, 1922; Singh Uberoi 1962), on the Gulf of Papua trade (Seligman 1910; Williams 1932; Groves 1960), on the systems of the central Solomons (H. I. Hogbin 1939) and the Huon Gulf (H. I. Hogbin 1947), and most recently on the extensive systems of the Vitiaz Strait area (Harding 1967). There were also trading systems in the eastern islands of the Fiji group (Thompson 1940; Sahlins 1962), between coastal and inland New Caledonia (Leenhardt 1937; Guiart 1963), between New Caledonia and the Loyalty Islands, along the coast of northern West Irian and extending into the northern Moluccas, and both within the central highlands of New Guinea and between this populated belt and the adjacent lowlands (e.g. Pospisil 1958, 1963; Dubbledam 1964; Nilles 1944, 1950; Meggitt 1958: 288-9; Veldkamp 1958; Reay 1959: 104-10; Brookfield and Brown 1963: 64-6). Even isolated Tikopia, almost without contact with the outside world, had 'rare barter of turmeric and food for a few manufactured products such as bows and arrows or turtle shell ornaments from Vanikoro and other islands to the north-west' (Firth 1939: 47), and some mention of pre-contact trading is found in almost every extended ethnological account of the western Pacific area. The Tolai of the Rabaul area of New Britain had a particularly well-developed system of local markets, trading mostly between coastal and inland ecological zones, and so organised that two markets were seldom held near each other on the same day (Epstein 1961: 7-8). By contrast, there seems to have been little regional trading in Polynesia except

11-52) and Dalton (1965). Polanyi distinguishes between reciprocity, as defined above, redistribution, designating 'appropriational movements towards a center and out of it again', and exchange, used to describe 'vice-versa movements taking place as between "hands" under a market system'. The latter term has not found general acceptance. The question of a surplus in subsistence production has been bandied back and forth for years, and Belshaw (1965:78) goes so far as to describe it as a 'red herring because only chance accident can produce a surplus over and above the planned expectations of the producer, who markets to obtain specific, needed, goals'. The matter is perhaps most successfully resolved by Allan's concept (1965:38-48) of a 'normal surplus' which arises in most years through planting sufficient to secure adequate subsistence in a poor year, and to accommodate unexpected demands on resources. In Allan's view it is this 'normal surplus' that is first used in market trading. See also Dalton (in press), for a major contribution to this discussion.

in larger archipelagos such as New Zealand and Hawaii (Fuchs 1961: 5); for Rarotonga, for example, Crocombe (1964: 19) specifically reports a complete absence of intra- or inter-island trade in pre-contact times.

Much of this trading took the form of direct barter, most characteristically of the products of one community against those of another. Harding (1967: 150-1) describes such a local 'market' between Siassi Island middlemen and people on Umboi in Vitiaz Strait in 1964:

> The meeting was prearranged. On the morning of the scheduled market, and all the day before, a procession of women transported taro to the beach . . . One Siassi canoe appeared just before noon. This canoe, with five crewmen, was nosed into the sand, and the exchange of fish and taro began immediately. On board this canoe was an Aramot Islander carrying a large wooden bowl, a small pot and a dog. This man later left the beach for the interior with his goods, though the pot was sold on the beach for tobacco.
>
> A second canoe arrived a half hour later and pulled up alongside the first one. Here again exchange commenced immediately. A crowd of chattering Kovai women waded into the water, placed several taro on the platform of the canoe, and eagerly held up their hands for several small fish in return. Each woman made a half-dozen or more dashes from her taro basket on the beach to the canoe, and the exchange was completed in less than fifteen minutes.
>
> In these exchanges there was hardly any discussion of the transactions themselves, though the women chattered and yelled incessantly. Two or three Siassi men squatted silently toward the rear of the canoe platforms doling out handfuls of fish each time several taro were placed before them . . . There was no haggling as such. A few times women were told to bring more taro, and the men tried to hurry the proceedings (the women were already running). Fish was exchanged first, then shellfish which had been removed from the shell. Each canoe ultimately received a half-dozen small baskets of taro for an equal number of baskets of fish and shellfish. Some of the shellfish was left over and was taken back home by the Mandoks. One packet of lime was also traded for tobacco.
>
> The main purpose of this meeting was not to exchange fish for taro, but to deliver large lots of taro in return for promised pigs. While the initial exchange of fish and taro was going on, large leaf packets of taro, weighing twenty-five to forty pounds each, were being piled up in groups of five and ten on the beach. Thirty of these packets, totalling about one-half ton of taro, were loaded onto the canoes by some of the men, while others discussed the transactions and decided upon future meetings. The entire proceedings lasted about an hour, and the canoes departed immediately.

Many of these systems contained elements of middleman trade, in which goods were traded through intermediaries to yield profit, especially in pigs. Middleman systems, integrated especially through the inhabitants of strategically placed small islands, were especially developed around Langalanga in the Solomons, Mailu in eastern Papua,

Siassi in Vitiaz Strait, Tami off the Huon peninsula, and Bilibili in Astrolabe Bay, near Madang (Harding 1967). Among these, only Siassi islanders survive as vigorous middleman traders today. A complex system, involving local, long-distance, and middleman trading, is well described for southwestern Papua early in the century, in these terms:

> There used to be regular markets . . . and now the Mawatta women sell fish almost daily to the bushwomen, who come down to the village for the purpose . . . One melon shell, to be used for making hoes, was worth forty bunches of bananas and ten baskets of taro. Ten pounds of fish bought a large bunch of bananas or about thirty pounds of taro . . .
>
> Partly owing to its situation and partly owing to the enterprising nature of its people, Mawatta has become an important trading centre, but acts more as a middleman than anything else. Many products are required by inland and river people that can only be obtained from the sea, and the people of the Torres Straits use many articles that can only be obtained in New Guinea.
>
> The principal article required for home consumption is food. Sago is largely bought from Kiwai Island, as Mawatta makes little or none of this commodity. From Torres Straits are imported such articles as shell armlets made from the *Conus millepunctatus*, pearl-shell crescents, dugong spears, nose shells, various shells used for all sorts of purposes and, in the old days, small pieces of iron . . . In return are traded drums, arrows, feathers, especially those of the *Paradisea raggiana*, boars' tusks and a little sago. A small amount of basketry and armlets and various earths to be used for pigments are exported from the Wassi-Kussa district principally through Boigu Island . . .
>
> The most important trade article affecting Mawatta and Turituri, however, is the canoe. Neither tribe are builders themselves, and they buy both for themselves and for the Torres Straits trade. As a rule Saibai used to buy from Mawatta and Murray and Darnley from Parama, but at the present day many of the Torres Straits buyers, after having received permission, buy direct from the Fly River traders . . . A large canoe is worth two large arm-shells and a small one, one melon shell, one dugong rib-bone, and a string of dogs' teeth. (Beaver 1920: 74-7)

This is commercial trading by any standards, with high value placed on rare commodities, and well-recognised equivalences. Probably more common, however, was the more diplomatic trading system of the Lau Islands in eastern Fiji, where emphasis lay in equal or better-than-equal giving, rather than on commerce:

> The most important export of Namuka is Tongan barkcloth. Most of it is traded to Lakemba in exchange for yams and taro; some is traded to Kambara for mats, kava and food bowls, and occasionally for a small canoe for use within the reef; a small amount finds its way to all the southern Lau islands except Ono (which produces sufficient Tongan barkcloth to supply her own demands). Namuka

also exports gongs, which go to Lakemba, Suva and Kambara and small canoes for lagoon use. Last year seven canoes were sent from Namuka to Lakemba, Matuku and Moala. Manioc, breadfruit, yams and bananas are traded to Fulanga and Ongea in return for mats and bowls; yams to Kambara in return for mats and bowls; to Komo and Mothe in return for food; sweet potatoes and watermelons (known as the best in Lau) to Lakemba . . .

Exchange is effected mainly by means of barter, although occasionally by the ceremonial prestation pattern. It is practically always carried out between relatives who act as hosts to the traders, housing and feeding them while they remain on the island. Goods are usually exchanged not singly but in piles. There are no fixed prices and there is no medium of exchange. First the initial payment or gift is made. The exchange is satisfactory if the return payment is 'levu' (big) for quantity is very important. Each transaction involves a unique adjustment between economic necessity and rivalry for social prestige on the part of traders. (Thompson 1940: 210-12)

Fijian trade was quite without currency, but various media of exchange were encountered in the western Pacific, from shells, teeth, and bones of only limited utilitarian value but acceptable in exchange, to shell currency of no value except as a medium of exchange. The persistence of this shell currency in the Rabaul area of New Britain is discussed at length by Epstein (1968), but shell was also acceptable in exchange for goods over large areas of inland New Guinea into modern times. Possibly the highest development of 'monetisation' of trade was among the Kapauku of the West Irian highlands, who amassed wealth in cowrie-shell money, and whose ceremonial feasts had as main object the bringing together of producers and buyers. At such an occasion:

From far and near people arrive carrying merchandise to be sold during the feast – which is at the same time a market – for other goods, shells or beads. Often these transactions are purely commercial, between strangers, and therefore non-recurrent. The selling of pork, however, may be different. Sellers of pork will try to make deals in advance with persons interested, who contract to buy a certain piece of meat in a future *juwo* [pig feast] when the buyers in their turn slaughter pigs. The carcasses are cut into pieces of standard sizes. Buyers offer a shell of standard size to the seller, who examines the shell critically and balances its value against that of the piece of meat desired. If the shell proves to be satisfactory, he will give the meat; if not he will return the shell. Hardly any word is spoken during the transaction, and only some hissing of approval or rejection made by the seller is heard when he is looking at the shell. It is also an important social event and a meeting place for all people who seek to meet others for some bargain or contract. (Dubbledam 1964: 297)

Major efforts were made to sustain the value of Kapauku cowrie-shell currency after European contact. When new shells began to be imported by Europeans in the 1930s the position of the old shells was protected by distinguishing between the old worn shells, which retained their value, and the new imports, which rapidly lost their value. However, the Kapauku were in trading contact with peoples who did not make this distinction, so it became possible for itinerant traders to obtain old shells for new at a very profitable rate. The quantity of 'old' shells in circulation in Kapauku was further increased by counterfeiting – making new shells look like old, initially by rubbing, later by immersing them in battery acid – and by the ageing of the early imports, so that by the 1950s a total devaluation set in. This undermined the position of the big men who – as among the Tolai – relied on their large shell holdings for their source of power, and enabled young and formerly powerless men to acquire wealth. It was these men who most readily seized the new opportunities, provided by labour and sale of produce, to make money.

The problem of 'equivalences' and variation in 'prices' in traditional trading systems has been tackled recently by Sahlins (1965), in a manner that is relevant to a discussion of modern markets. He is not concerned with the 'monetised' trading systems so much as with those in which equivalence depended on equal giving (or equality-with-good-measure) between trading partners. To simplify does some damage to the intricacies of his argument, but it seems he sees the key to his problems in the fact that reciprocal exchange is an arrangement between individuals, so that it is the social relationship of exchange partnership, not the price mechanism, which provides the means of access to goods, a relationship that would be destroyed if buyers and sellers were to compete freely for each other's business:

> Perhaps more important, where such customary [exchange] rates prevail, and especially where trade is organised by partnerships, there are alternative strategies to competitive undercutting which do not involve the material disadvantages of lowering selling prices or raising offers: one alternative is to acquire more trade connections with whom one deals at prevailing rates; another is to overpay one's partner for the time being, which obliges him to reciprocate within a reasonable time on pain of losing face or partnership, thus completing the transaction at the usual ratio. No question that there may be competition for volume of trade: internal prestige systems often hinge on it. But it does not develop as price-manipulation, product differentiation, or the like. The standard maneuver is to get additional outside partners, or else step up trade with existing partners. (Sahlins 1965: 102-3)

Despite their differences, indigenous trading systems have certain elements in common. Goods are handled in units of standard size, with known equivalences that do not vary in the short term, except by deliberate overpayment in order to obligate a trading partner to reciprocate. Where such practices are adopted, they are directly against the trading partner, and do not constitute competition among either sellers or buyers. Access to goods is valued above the profit motive, though advantageously placed traders – operating as a group against buyers as a group – could and did take large profits where they had a monopoly of supply. Middlemen could find niches in some systems, but not in others, but again they operated as groups rather than as individuals. There is little or no haggling, and an unsatisfactory exchange is simply rejected. On the other hand there is quite extensive use of 'credit', both in the form of delayed exchanges, and, in some 'monetised' systems, of specific loans at high interest. Inevitably, credit is a major source of dissatisfaction. The motivation for trading cannot be seen as wholly economic; where there are no sharp differentials in living standards within or between societies, the essential motivation is prestige and ambition to leadership and influence; trade partners stand in the relation of kin so that:

> The trade system is a vast interpersonal network. Traders do not maneuver in relation to the demand of an indefinitely large group of buyers or customers, but are restricted to a small number of social contacts. For individual traders the market is expandable only to a limited extent and along lines of kinship – the kindred of trade friends. In addition, demand in the immediate sense is phrased as a personal need. The obligation to satisfy the wants and needs of the trade friends is matched on other occasions by the obligation to accept whatever trade friends have to offer. (Harding 1967: 243)

With the possible exception only of the highly monetised and individualised system of the Kapauku, these generalisations would apply not only to formal pre-contact trading as found in the western Pacific, but also to the institutionalised exchanges found throughout the Pacific. This is the context into which modern forms of trade made entry, and the background against which these modern forms have found adoption.

The growth of market-place trading in the colonial period

New goods brought in by Europeans were initially traded within the traditional systems, but as their quantity increased, old levels of equivalence became strained, leading to the rupture of trade partnerships. Some trading systems were destroyed by the demands of Europeans for land and labour, which broke up the finely-balanced systems, destroying niches, finding other work for the members. Others have declined as new forms of gaining access to wealth have appeared through cash cropping, and sale of goods and labour to the newcomers. At the same time, new opportunities for substantial profit-taking were opened up for people able to acquire new goods cheaply and sell them expensively, or to travel through formerly hostile areas and cut out the intermediaries who formerly made a profit on the trade. Devaluation both of formerly scarce goods and of media of exchange, such as cowrie shells, affected the systems in a variety of ways. As trading partnerships based on stable comparative costs between different areas became untenable, they were dissolved. In institutionalised exchanges not primarily connected with trade, on the other hand, the value of some goods in relatively inelastic supply, such as pigs, increased sharply in terms of the old exchange media, so that as these were devalued they were replaced by money, and money could be obtained only by participation in the new economy. Further, as increase in the supply of money forced up the value of scarce items needed for institutionalised exchanges, inflation led to a demand for money which exceeded its ready supply. Where traditional exchange systems were not discontinued but rather increased in scale through competitive or hostile bidding up, a strong pressure of demand for money developed. Differentials in the demand for money in the Pacific may thus bear some relation to the nature of indigenous systems of reciprocal trade and exchange.

Initially, newcomers had two effects: first, they brought new goods, which they were prepared to exchange for native foodstuffs; second, they did not enter the existing system as exchange partners, but introduced a new and impersonal form of trade. Generally, throughout the Pacific, it was customary for trading parties to be fed by the people whose territory they visited, and early European parties sometimes received gifts of food in the same way. These were generally reciprocated in kind, with axes, knives, beads, and the like, and – in some inland areas – with shell, especially cowrie shell. But visits were not arranged, and partnerships not continued; second visitors were seldom received so hospitably as the first, and reactions were sometimes ambiguous. Late in the history of exploration, McCarthy led a patrol to establish the first government post in the Kukukuku country of central New Guinea, an area already penetrated by gold prospectors. An attempt was made to kill the party at its first camp-site, and immediately after their failure the same men

> were now beginning to make their way down – waving cheerfully. We saw that they now had with them large bilums of sweet potatoes and sugar – and five minutes later trading commenced . . . Both these tribes brought us food, for they were desperately anxious for our steel knives and axes. (McCarthy 1963: 118)

Such initial naivety soon gave way to keener valuation of equivalences. The first party through the Chimbu country in 1933 was overwhelmed with gifts of food, but by 1934 the Leahys were already having difficulties. On their third passage they turned away ten pigs offered for sale because the Chimbu were demanding two goldlip shells or a goldlip shell plus an axe (Leahy 1930-4: 2 April 1934). Valuation of foodstuffs developed quickly in all areas by diffusion of example, and not without some forms of bargaining. Bulmer (1962: 17) reports the experience of a party of Chimbu plume traders at Yaramanda in the Western Highlands of New Guinea in 1955:

> The headman, a pagan, did not criticise the trade as such, but nevertheless made a speech, which he had translated to the traders, to the effect that it was traditional among his people to offer food freely to visiting strangers; however, he said, some youths from Yaramanda had recently walked through Chimbu territory while travelling in search of work, and had had to pay 1s. for a meal of a few sweet potatoes, and therefore the Chimbu themselves should expect to pay for the food that they were given. The assistant headman meanwhile sent a youth to fetch a bunch of cooking bananas. The Chimbu leader ostentatiously gave him 9d. for it. The general opinion at Yaramanda was that the Chimbu were bad, dishonest people.

Once strangers settled permanently at a place regular equivalences were speedily reached. 'Government', wrote Beaver (1920: 254), 'has a habit of saying "Here are twenty police and six months' stores. Go and open a Station".' The stores would consist of such things as imported rice and bully beef, kerosene, and the like, together with a supply of trade goods with which to establish a regular supply of fresh foodstuffs, and to pay for the necessary local labour. In a way, these stations were like visiting trading parties permanently settled at one place, seeking the produce of the country rather than specialised goods of known value, but providing specialised goods in return. Other things came with the goods, such as orders and policing from government, Christianity from the missions, demands for land and labour from the planters, and all were exacting in their demands on indigenous behaviour. But the commercial relationship of buyer and seller was a common and continuing element; here at least was something that had to be paid for at a negotiated price.

With the emergence of a non-agricultural sector following pacification and development, it is surprising that the Pacific market-place did not develop in its modern form much more rapidly than it did, and that a redistribution and enlargement of trading systems did not take place, focusing on the towns, plantations, and outstations. Even at Rabaul, where the growth of this form of trade is better documented than at most places, and where there was already an extensive system of periodic rural produce markets, change was slow. In 1911 it was reported that the Tolai were selling vegetables to plantations, sometimes through European middlemen (Germany 1910-11), but the old system persisted into the 1920s, when:

> In Rabaul and elswhere [in the surrounding district] native markets are frequently to be observed where considerable numbers of natives congregate with their produce. In some cases the market places are merely a spot by the wayside on a coconut plantation, and they exist

> as market places only on account of native use and custom. Even in the township of Rabaul no provision has been made to accommodate the market in a suitable place or building. (Commonwealth of Australia 1924-5: 29)

On the urging of the Department of Agriculture, a market building was erected in Rabaul in 1928 (Commonwealth of Australia 1927-8: 59), and this market-place grew swiftly to be one of the largest and most active in the Pacific (Epstein 1961). But until World War II most goods could still be had even there for tobacco, and the use of money did not become general until after 1945.

There are a number of obvious explanations for this general lag. Expatriate populations continued to depend on imported foods, even in days when refrigerators were almost unknown.

> One of the difficulties [of life for Europeans in the pre-war Pacific] . . . is the monotony of the food. In some of the towns, or on plantations which keep cattle, fresh meat is obtainable, and sometimes fresh milk and butter. But as a rule tinned foods are the staple. Vegetables of European type are generally scarce, and, though native vegetables can often be had, they are commonly regarded as inferior. In most areas, attempts have been made in recent years to improve the supply of vegetables, but the climate does not favour European varieties. Contrary to what one might expect, fish does not appear on the menu a great deal, partly from conservatism in organising supplies and partly because even on the coast it is not always easy to obtain. Cooking for Europeans is done as a rule by natives, whose imagination and training have usually given them only a limited range of recipes. (NID 1945: 360-1)

Nor did only the Europeans depend on imported food: until quite recent years the overwhelming majority of all native and Asian employees of European enterprises and government were supplied with quarters, clothing, and rations. In the early days these consisted overwhelmingly of rice; later, after medical advisers began to remark on the high incidence of malnutrition symptoms among labourers, the diet was varied with additional supplies of tinned meat, fat, sugar, and the like. It was possible for employers to supplement these rations, or partly replace them, with locally bought native foods, but several forces acted against any large-scale substitution. It was difficult to ensure a regular supply at the level required, and whereas native supplies had to be bought in cash, imported goods could be had on account: since most planters were in debt to the companies, the companies which bought the copra also expected the planter to buy his supplies from the same source. Cash wages were small, and few unskilled men were paid more than $2 per month except in Fiji and New Caledonia. In rural areas much of this was spent in plantation trade stores, and in the towns and outstations at Chinese stores. Comparatively little of the wages and salaries paid either to expatriates or to natives thus went to local producers.

As a result, and despite the major changes of the post-1945 period, a remarkable feature of the supply of vegetables, fruit, meat, and dairy produce to the Pacific islands is the large sector of the market that is supplied from Australia and New Zealand, especially the former. This developed early and has persisted. Developments in snap-freezing and refrigeration in the past twenty years have made it possible to transport fruit and European vegetables for sale in near-fresh condition in all centres served by the main shipping routes, or by air services from the ports. Even milk can now be preserved for long-distance transport, without refrigeration, and though this process has not yet been adopted extensively there is now no technical reason why Australian or New Zealand milk should not be exportable throughout the Pacific. Australian and New Zealand foods are expensive, but are regarded as 'safe' by the Europeans, and as a source of prestige by the natives; in areas poor in local production, such as New Caledonia and the Port Moresby area of Papua, even the price differential is less significant. With an expanding market for produce, a large share of demand has continued to go to imported produce, to the benefit of Australasian export trade to the islands, controlled and retailed mainly through the commercial houses, but to the detriment of the local market-place. The effect of this competition is here seen very clearly at Vila; it is still more marked at Nouméa.

There has, none the less, been a major expansion of Pacific market-place trade since World War II, as a direct consequence first of the rapid growth of towns, second of new directions in government policy, and third of the efforts of much enlarged agricultural extension services. While population figures on Pacific towns, especially of indigenous and Asian inhabitants, are so deficient as to be almost useless until recent years, it is clear that urban populations in all territories have increased by several hundred per cent, and that some towns are now growing at rates as high as 10 per cent per year. Since 1940, Port Moresby has increased from some 5,000 to 45,000, Suva from under 20,000 to 50,000, Nouméa from 11,000 to 37,000, Papeete from 12,000 to 42,000, Vila from 1,000 to 5,000, Honiara from nothing to 7,000, and so on. In addition, a large number of new towns have come into existence, especially in Papua-New Guinea, while elsewhere such small but growing towns as Gizo and Auki (Solomons), Santo (New Hebrides), Nadi (Fiji), Avarua (Rarotonga), and Betio (Tarawa, Gilbert and Ellice Islands) have risen from little or nothing since 1945.

These new urban populations are different from the pre-war urban populations not only in size but also in nature. European populations have grown, and there has emerged in every Pacific town of any size a resident indigenous population, working for wages or engaged in various entrepreneurial activities. To the employed population is often added a large floating population of visitors, some seeking work or between jobs, others merely looking around. Asian population groups have also become more urbanised as the former tie of most of them to rural employment has ended. At the same time wages have risen sharply, and are generally much higher in town than in the country, and the 'rationing' of employees ceased first and most completely in the towns.

The consequence of all these changes is a major increase in the demand for foodstuffs, though this has been shared perhaps unequally between the overseas supplies handled mainly through the shops and the locally-grown supplies handled – in most areas – through the market-place. Urban produce markets have grown much larger, and many new markets have sprung up in smaller towns. In the New Guinea highlands, where coffee was established as a cash crop in 1954, marketing of produce was still the main source of cash income in 1960. At Goroka, which lies in the centre of the first main coffee-growing area, a produce market was set up in 1957; income from coffee did not exceed income from sweet potato sales until after 1960 (Howlett 1962: 100-2). In Chimbu, which now produces some 20 per cent of New Guinea's coffee crop, income from coffee was estimated at only $2,000 in 1960, while income from the sale of vegetables and sweet potatoes for the whole Sub-district was estimated at about $4,000, even in the absence of regular markets. The rapid growth of new markets is here documented in the substantive cases of Popondetta and Kerema. There has also been some re-emergence of rural periodic markets in wholly native areas, bringing the old trade between contrasted ecological zones into a modern cash-using framework. Such marketing has grown up between coastal villages and villages of the Middle Bush in Tanna, New Hebrides. On Umboi in Vitiaz Strait. Harding (1967:218-19) reports the success of a government-sponsored market-place established for similar purposes in 1964 at a village a little inland from the coast.

Government action has played an important part in this recent expansion of market-place trade. Lasaqa here recounts in some detail the example of Honiara, where special action was necessary. Seeds were widely distributed, and advice on market gardening given by extension officers. The hand of government was also present in the establishment of market-places at Kerema and Popondetta, and at numerous other small places, though there has been no such aid at Vila and Apia. There has, however, been little comprehensive planning for market gardening, and while much sustained effort has gone into the development of indigenous export crops, encouragement of market gardening has been at best sporadic, and for the most part *laissez faire*.

This applies especially to the possibilities of replacing imports of fresh, frozen, and canned vegetables of the European type by local produce. In the more southerly islands, and in the large populated areas above 2,500 feet in the northern islands, there is no doubt that all these commodities would grow well: the central highlands of New Guinea could certainly supply all the fruit and vegetables required in the country, given adequate organisation for marketing and transport. Low backhaul rates on cargo aircraft returning to the coastal port-cities offer a fast, reliable, and relatively cheap means of carriage. Some missions have gone into business on their own account, and some European entrepreneurs also attempted to develop this business, but there has been no consistent organisation. In the Baliem valley of West Irian, at 5,000 feet, police and one Eurasian settler were encouraged to plant vegetables for shipment to Hollandia in 1958, and within months these were being grown by the newly contacted highland people and brought to the airstrip for sale. Hollandia (Sukarnapura) had no other reliable source of supply. This traffic continues under the Indonesians (Iskandar 1964). In Australian New Guinea, the people of the Chimbu area were encouraged to plant cabbages and onions; they did so extensively in the expectation of large sales, but a year later most of these unsaleable crops had gone to seed or been pulled out of the ground. There is a small sale of central-highland and mountain Papuan produce in Port Moresby, which, being in a semi-arid area, has a serious and perennial shortage of supplies.

No attempts have hitherto been made to offer any special protection to local producers of vegetables, fruit, and other fresh produce in Australian and New Zealand territories, or in British territories with close commercial ties with Australia. This is a complex problem, as may be seen in the somewhat different circumstances of Fiji and New Caledonia. In Fiji, Spate (1959: 48) reports the fate of a serious attempt to organise potato production through co-operative societies in the Sigatoka valley. A good contract was secured at a price of $45 per ton, but supply proved uneven as *colporteurs* were able to buy potatoes at lower prices but for spot cash. Reliance on imported potatoes continues. The Burns Commission argued that Fijian producers were holding out for prices at which it was cheaper for the colony to import from other territories, and that the price of taro, cassava, and *yaqona* (kava) was particularly high: taro, at four to five Fijian shillings per bundle, was in effect priced at up to $134 per ton, while potatoes could be landed in Suva at $60 per ton (Burns, Watson, and Peacock 1960: 50). In New Caledonia quite extreme forms of protection have been offered to the local producers with very little beneficial effect. These measures have included not only high import tariffs but also total prohibitions on imports when local production satisfies demand, often imposed at very short notice. Angleviel (1961), Demene (1962), and Pisier (1962) have argued that New Caledonian agriculture never reorganised itself after a short period of rapid expansion to supply the exceptional demand of the wartime period. Agriculture is highly mechanised – with one tractor per 37 acres under cultivation, New Caledonian agriculture is more highly mechanised than that of the United States (Le Borgne 1964: 176). During recent years some pattern has developed, and market gardening is no longer important in distant parts of the island, but there continue to be wild swings in prices, and great lack of co-ordination between production and imports. In 1960 New Caledonia produced only 1,400 tons of vegetables against 759 tons fresh and 1,370 tons preserved imported from Australia (Angleviel 1961). Though McTaggart (1963: 81) pointed out that Angleviel's figures do not take account of the mainly Vietnamese production in and around urban Nouméa, this general picture has not greatly changed. In potatoes, especially, imports continue to be as great as local production, and the cost of imported goods is below the Nouméa price for a variety of vegetables (Tonnelier *et al.* 1966: 22-3). Vegetable and potato production continue to oscillate wildly from year to year, and fruit production remains as described by Pisier (1962: 53) – gathering rather than agriculture. The high cost of labour contributes to the uncertainties of New Caledonian agriculture.

In French Polynesia, on the other hand, an attempt to stimulate vegetable production by offering a guaranteed market met with some success. Since 1945 the economy of Tahiti and neighbouring islands has been transformed by the rapid growth of Papeete, which now has half the whole territorial population. Finney (1965a, 1965b) has described the transformation of peasants near Papeete into a wage-earning proletariat, buying food for daily meals – even traditional staples – in the urban market. Severe shortages were experienced, despite a well-organised market-place, and in 1961 the government guaranteed to buy all fruit and vegetables offered from a number of islands in the Austral group at fixed, if low, prices, itself arranging transport to Papeete and sale on the urban market. The operation ran at a loss in 1961 and 1962, but made a profit in 1963; some transport was provided on naval vessels and not costed. In 1964 the scheme was extended to supply the military in the Tuamotu Islands from the remote Gambier group, using naval transport entirely (Doumenge 1966: 391-2). Such extreme measures as this, however, are not for general application.

An interpretation of indigenous trading practices in the market-places

It is as well to recall at this point the brief review of the characteristics of Pacific market-place trading offered earlier, specifying especially those characteristics that are common to indigenous traders in all the markets reviewed here, but not so much to non-indigenous traders. First is the general practice of selling by quantities, not by weight, and in lots offered at fixed prices which are most commonly of 10 cents or one shilling, or multiples of this unit. In Rabaul market, though not elsewhere, there is some continuing use of shell money; 11 per cent of all transactions, but about 25 per cent of intra-Tolai transactions, were made in this traditional medium (Epstein 1961: 15). At Vila, sixpenny and threepenny coins (5 cents and 2·5 cents) were used in 1965, but pennies and single francs were of little service; paper money was used rather more extensively than in other markets. At Kerema, betel nuts alone were sold retail for pennies, all else in shillings, while at Honiara nothing was sold for less than 10 cents, but many goods were sold in one dollar (ten shilling) lots. This simplification of currency has obvious advantages and there are historical reasons. Money was paid to Pacific islanders from the earliest times in silver coinage, and small change has only recently become acceptable to indigenes. In New Guinea, territorial shillings were for long punched with a central hole so that they could be threaded on a string, like shell money.

The use of silver currency has obvious compatibility with pre-contact concepts of equivalence rates. Then, as now, small goods were generally offered in bundles, seldom individually, and never by variable weight or other standard of measure, and equivalences were not generally required for units smaller than such bundles. The quantity included in such bundles or parcels was variable, and the main problem in obtaining equivalences lay in this variation, whether the exchange was by direct barter or was delayed. Except that the introduction of silver coinage removed the possibility of variation in the quality of exchange media – always present with shells – the modern method of judging equivalences has a direct link with indigenous and ancient practice.

There are other elements of continuity between reciprocal and market trading. Sellers generally congregate together in market-places in village groups, just as they would at a ceremonial prestation. The 'visitors' – buyers – now come as individuals, but the sellers form a group even though trading as individuals. As Sahlins (1965) stresses, absence of within-group competition was an important element in traditional trading and in prestations generally. Goods rejected in a traditional trading meeting would be taken away by the vendor, as they are in the market; attempts to make a sale by unilateral price reduction involve an element of competition which is destructive of the competitive strength of the group as a whole.

Here we approach the central complex of problems: absence of competition, passive waiting for a sale, reluctance to reduce prices late in the day, the practice of each seller offering her own produce, refusal to haggle. Epstein (1961: 5-10) discussed these problems at some length, giving weight to the range of interpersonal kinship ties linking people throughout the market in relationships of mutual dependence. These social factors, in various forms, are widespread in the Pacific. Marketing practices are also similar. They appear instantly in a new market such as that established at Barang on Umboi in 1964: Harding (1967: 218) attributes the similarity to modelling the new market on town market practices. At Apia and Vila, where there is some competitive variation in size of bundles, the main variation is only between separated parts of the market; the general pattern is modified only in degree.

Since common marketing practices are so widespread, may we not also seek a partial explanation in economic terms? By maintaining a relatively uniform price structure, refusing to haggle, avoiding competition within the sellers' group, and being prepared to take produce away or destroy it rather than accept what is regarded as an insufficient price, sellers are in some measure acting in their own long-term interest. Though refusing to bargain *ad hoc* and as individuals, they are collectively bargaining for the maintenance of established equivalences, and using the tools of collective bargaining in order to do so. Hence the evil looks which Lasaqa's price-cutting Malaitan received from his Tasimboko co-vendors at Honiara; here was an outsider, a blackleg, spoiling things for the others. Dakeyne's schoolchildren who could buy vegetables for salt in Popondetta were perhaps being treated generously because of their position: it would be interesting to know if this continued for very long.

Let us consider the possible effects of short-term price variation on demand and supply. The total quantities of all produce which each individual seller can bring to market, or which each individual buyer is able to consume, are both limited, and no amount of price variation can do much to stretch these limits. If an individual seller reduces his price, he may sell his produce more quickly, but he would reap no long-term advantage from doing so. Not only would competitive price reduction become general, but no individual, while continuing to operate as an individual producer-seller, would be able to increase his supply in response to any resultant increase in demand; thus he would obtain only a lower income from future sales. Such considerations may not be present in the minds of the sellers, but this would be the effect. With regard to demand, the situation is even more complex. Produce markets are in competition with trade stores and entertainments for the available money, but they do not supply the same range of commodities. Since in Pacific towns there is no large proletarian population that is presently too poor to pay for the basic foodstuffs it requires, a fall in price would not necessarily create a larger demand for produce-market goods; instead, clothes and luxuries, bought from the trade-stores, might be substituted in the expenditure pattern.[4] Within the produce market, fruit and European vegetables are much more amenable to demand substitution through cross-elasticities than are native staples, and hence are more variable in price, as Epstein noted (1961: 9), and as emerges here also at Kerema, Apia, Honiara, and Vila. The elasticity of demand is greater for European vegetables than for native staple foods; price reduction in the latter might merely lead to increase in substitution.

Since most goods are sold by individual producers and bought by individual consumers, the principal short-term means of variation in demand and supply is simply an increase or decrease in the number of buyers and sellers – especially the latter. As in the traditional markets, these variations operate by increasing or decreasing the number of 'trading partners' rather than by varying the equivalence rates. Changes in prices do take place in the long term, both by a form of progressive collective bargaining, and by addition to or subtraction from the market of sellers whose basic acceptable return is higher or lower. But this economic reasoning is upset by the fact that the utility of a market visit cannot be measured only by the cash returns obtained. Many sellers visit town for social purposes, to buy goods in the shops, to make deals, and often for several purposes combined. This is perhaps especially true of those vendors who bring only small quantities to market – just enough to defray the costs of the journey if they are lucky enough to make a sale, not so much as will prove an embarrassment if they are unsuccessful.

The behaviour of indigenous sellers can be explained rationally, but a rationale emerges only with the recognition that it is not everyone's aim to maximise individual profit at each market trip, and that a proportion of sellers attend the market only to defray costs of a visit to town for other purposes. Among indigenous sellers, there are few who depend primarily on the market-place for a livelihood. Wage employment, perennial cash crops, and operations within the local economy are available to almost all. This is far less true of the Asian migrants who participate in a number of the markets, many of whom have little land, usually rent what they have, and have no village-based subsistence economy as a secure foundation for their activities. Some Pacific island migrants, such as the Malaitans at Honiara, are also in this position, and in an analogous but not identical situation are the mixed-blood people of Samoa and the New Hebrides, who by the nature of their

[4] Demene (1962) notes that this occurs even in Nouméa, with its mainly European population.

land rights have a greater stake in the commercial economy. These latter groups display more competitive practices, readiness to vary prices and to sell in small lots, greater sensitivity to demand, and a stronger profit motive. The part-Samoans at Apia, the mainly Vietnamese 'core group' at Vila, the Malaitans at Honiara, are the pace-setters of more commercial practices in the Pacific markets. In a sense, these people stand between the group-structured Pacific island traders and the riotous individualism of markets in Asia and the Caribbean.

The realm of the carrier, middleman, and colporteur

The question of the hinterlands of Pacific market-places is discussed in the concluding chapter, but it will be readily apparent from the data here presented on Honiara and Vila in particular that an important and profitable role in market operation is played by the carriers – Chinese shipowners and Fiji-Indian truck operators at Honiara, New Hebridean and formerly Vietnamese taxi operators at Vila. A substantial part of the profits of market trading is eaten up by transport costs, especially where every seller travels to market with his or her own produce.

The carriers are in a fortunate position, for they bear little or none of the risk, take an assured payment whether or not the goods are sold, and, if they hold a monopoly over means of transport that are in short supply, can successfully charge whatever the traffic will bear. This is especially so where, as is often the case, they are not local people enmeshed in a net of interpersonal obligations. Around some markets much of the carriage is done in locally-owned vehicles; this is the case at Rabaul, and Lasaqa notes the beginnings of locally-owned transport east of Honiara. In other markets, however, the carriers not only carry, but also buy and sell produce on their own account: these *colporteurs* and middlemen are hardly represented in this collection at all.

Market middlemen, who buy on their own account for resale, are only rarely to be found among indigenous traders in Pacific markets. Epstein (1961: 4) notes some little development of this kind at Rabaul, but her 'middleman-women' buy goods in the market to hawk around the town, not for resale in the market itself. This is also done at Port Moresby, and perhaps elsewhere in the larger New Guinea markets, but it is nowhere there an important field of indigenous enterprise.

It is otherwise in Fiji, where the produce markets are dominated by Indian traders, but with a growing proportion of Fijians. There were markets on plantations in Fiji early in the century, modelled on Indian bazaars, and wholly concerned with trade between Indians. Specialised salesmen traded in sweetmeats, *yaqona* (kava), tobacco, vegetables, fowls, and goats; and jewellers, tailors, and barbers also plied their trade in the Saturday markets (Burton 1910: 295-302). The modern market-places at Suva, Lautoka, Nadi, Ba, Labasa, and smaller places are all dominated by Indians, and are an amalgam of men and women who grow and market their own produce, and of market middlemen, with the latter more and more important. The main producing area of market garden produce in Fiji is within twenty miles of Suva, and much produce from these specialised farms is sold in Suva by the growers, both in the market and to shops. Other producers sell their goods to middlemen at the market; thus the people of Beqa Island, twenty-five miles from Suva, operate launches in which they take bananas, yams, tomatoes, and other produce to the landing in Nubukalau Creek by the Suva Municipal Market, where they sell it to the market stall-holders (Couper 1967: 204). Much the same is done from the Yasawas and Mamanuca Islands to Lautoka:

> Contact with Lautoka is maintained by a fleet of locally built cutters, many of which are now fitted with outboard engines. People travel in with the cutters in order to sell copra, coconuts, yams, breadfruit, bananas, *lai ros* (land crabs), dried fish, fowls, goats, mats and *voivoi*. The cutters are overloaded with passengers and produce on the way to Lautoka, and are equally so on the return trip to the islands, when they contain quantities of building material, benzine, store goods, second-hand furniture and *yaqona*. Passengers pay a fare of from $1.50 to $3 for the round trip and copra is charged at a rate of 60 cents per bag . . .
>
> Marketing at Lautoka takes several forms. Fresh produce, fowls and goats are often sold to Indian market middlemen on the beach, or the fresh produce is bought by Fijians who meet the boats (often stevedores loading sugar ships). Some people carry the produce they have brought in from the islands to the municipal market and there sell them to a stall-holder. Others, almost invariably women, will sit on the ground in a group at the market to sell fresh produce, crabs and coconuts. (Couper 1967: 205-6)

In addition to these stall-holding market middlemen, who buy and sell goods at the market-place itself, there is also in Fiji, as in the African and central American markets, an important group of *colporteurs* who buy produce in the rural area on their own account, and transport it either to market, or to another middleman located at some intermediate point. These men have a stake in the transport of the not inconsiderable volume of produce which reaches the urban markets from quite remote areas. The head of the Sigatoka valley is 100 miles by road from Suva, 70 from Nadi, 90 from Lautoka, 110 from Ba, but all these markets are supplied from the valley by road. From the opening of the valley road in 1953 Indians began hiring trucks, purchasing produce from Fijian and Indian farmers, and retailing in the markets. Within a year some Fijians were doing the same (Belshaw 1964: 103-4).

> Most farmers prepared their produce on Friday morning . . . Horses and punts brought produce across the river . . . Indian and Fijian

> farmers brought horse and bullock drawn sleds packed with bananas, tapioca and corn; women gathered cress from the nearby streams and lugged it to the road in dripping sacks; middlemen visited gardens and picked over tomatoes as the growers gathered them; others carefully examined beans, melons, pumpkins. There was much haggling over prices and argument over quality, and merrymaking as girls flirted with young men embarking on the marketing adventure, Indian drivers and entrepreneurs exchanged cigarettes with Fijian 'tavale' [essentially trade-partners in this context], and village women gossiped with buyers who had come down from other villages. Finally, the produce was loaded, and the trucks sped away to the towns. Sometimes they did not leave till night, loading under the light of headlamps; a wise driver kept off the road on Fridays to avoid the hasty convoys. In the towns, middlemen dossed down where they could with friends or on the trucks, spent some of their business capital on food and drink and sold in the jostling throngs of Saturday morning. With afternoon came the reckoning; the purchase of the material goods that motivated the profit; a visit to the cinema, the boxing match, or the gamblers . . . .

With a mark-up seldom much below 100 per cent, this could be a profitable business, with a credit balance to show even after 'selling expenses', which included the pleasures of town life. But the field is limited because of keen competition among *colporteurs*, while some growers take their own produce to town, and a few specialists operating on a larger scale make regular deliveries to urban middlemen on their own account. This is marketing practice far removed from the multiplicity of small producer-traders visiting Rabaul, Kerema, or even Honiara and Apia, squatting quietly behind their produce, careful to avoid the appearance of competition: Fijian haggling is within limits defined by the calls of politeness, and by the need to keep trade relationships both open and sweet, but without question Fijian middleman trade and *colportage* is business, and the pity is that we yet know so little about it.

Even more purely commercial, if far less satisfactory in its results, is the *colportage* of New Caledonia. The two main buyers of fresh produce in New Caledonia are Nouméa city and the mines, the former by far the more important. Nouméa is in a very dry area, remote from closely settled native populations because the nearby natives were mostly removed from their land by very drastic methods in the second half of the nineteenth century, so that a dependence on Australian supplies which began in those early days has persisted down to the present time. There is a recently rebuilt central produce market in Nouméa, and a separate meat market, but most produce reaches the consumer in this predominantly European town through retail stores, and a little by means of hawkers. From early in the present century until 1942 fresh vegetables were grown on plots of land in the environs of Nouméa by Japanese market gardeners and hawked around the town. The 105 market gardeners were exempted from internment applied to all other Japanese in 1941, but in 1942 the Governor acceded to the demands of the newly arrived Americans that these too be placed behind bars (Sautot 1949: 138). Later they were deported and their property confiscated: such of their gardens as have not subsequently been built over were continued by Vietnamese. But this peri-urban supply has never been sufficient, and has been supplemented first by both European and native supplies from the area of Paita, thirty miles away, and later from the agricultural areas on alluvial land at La Foa and Bourail, which supplied about half the small amount of vegetable produce, potatoes, and cereals grown a few years ago (Angleviel 1961; Demene 1962). Latterly there has been an increase in the amount of vegetable production close to Nouméa, and most of this is sold in the market by the producers (Tonnelier *et al.* 1966: 13-25).

Most of the remoter supply, however, is sold through *colporteurs*, who buy from the producers and resell in Nouméa, sometimes in the market, sometimes through the large stores, sometimes to the retail shops. Opinions differ on the efficiency of this system: some criticise it severely on the grounds that selection and packing are often poor, and that when the city is overstocked, *colporteurs* may even fail to turn up to buy the produce, resulting in a complete loss of the crop. Others argue that the *colporteur* is difficult to replace, since he combines an intimate knowledge of the producing areas with a close understanding of the market (Tonnelier *et al.* 1966: 26).

The one case of middleman business we have here is that of Ho, the Vietnamese middleman who occupies a central place in more senses than one in the market at Vila. The uniqueness and small scale of this example, in contrast to the scale of the middleman business in New Caledonian, Fijian, and Tahitian marketing is indicative of the unbalanced state of present research on produce marketing in the Pacific. If one may conclude this introductory essay with a suggestion, it is that attention should be given not only to the indigenous markets and indigenous peri-urban situations but also to those places, mostly dominated by non-indigenes of one kind or another, where something more akin to the complex and highly commercial situations of Asia and middle-America already exists in the Pacific.

II

The Small Market at Popondetta, Northern Papua

R. B. Dakeyne

Popondetta is the administrative centre for the Northern District. It is a very new and immature township, having grown from a mission station and one trade store in 1951 to its present population of 2,139 (1,845 indigenes and 294 Europeans) at the time of the mid-1966 census. Before World War II the District Administration headquarters was located at Buna on the coast; after the war it was established at Higaturu, on a little plateau 1,000 feet above sea-level on the slopes of Mt Lamington. Higaturu was completely destroyed and all its residents killed in the volcanic eruption of Mt Lamington on 21 January 1951. The Administration then decided on Popondetta, 12 miles north of Higaturu, as the site for its District headquarters.

The Northern District comprises four Sub-districts; Popondetta, Kokoda, Ioma, and Tufi; of these Popondetta Sub-district, with 26,000 people (in 1960), is easily the most populous. It is also the scene of most economic activity in the District, and as a result, is better served by air services and roads than any other Sub-district; the main port for the District, Cape Killerton, is thirteen miles northeast of Popondetta township. Map 2 indicates the central location of Popondetta township in its Sub-district; population densities are shown by census division within Popondetta Sub-district.

A weekly market has been held regularly on Saturday mornings at Popondetta since 1956. It is now an important institution in the lives of the townspeople and of the surrounding villagers, functioning as it

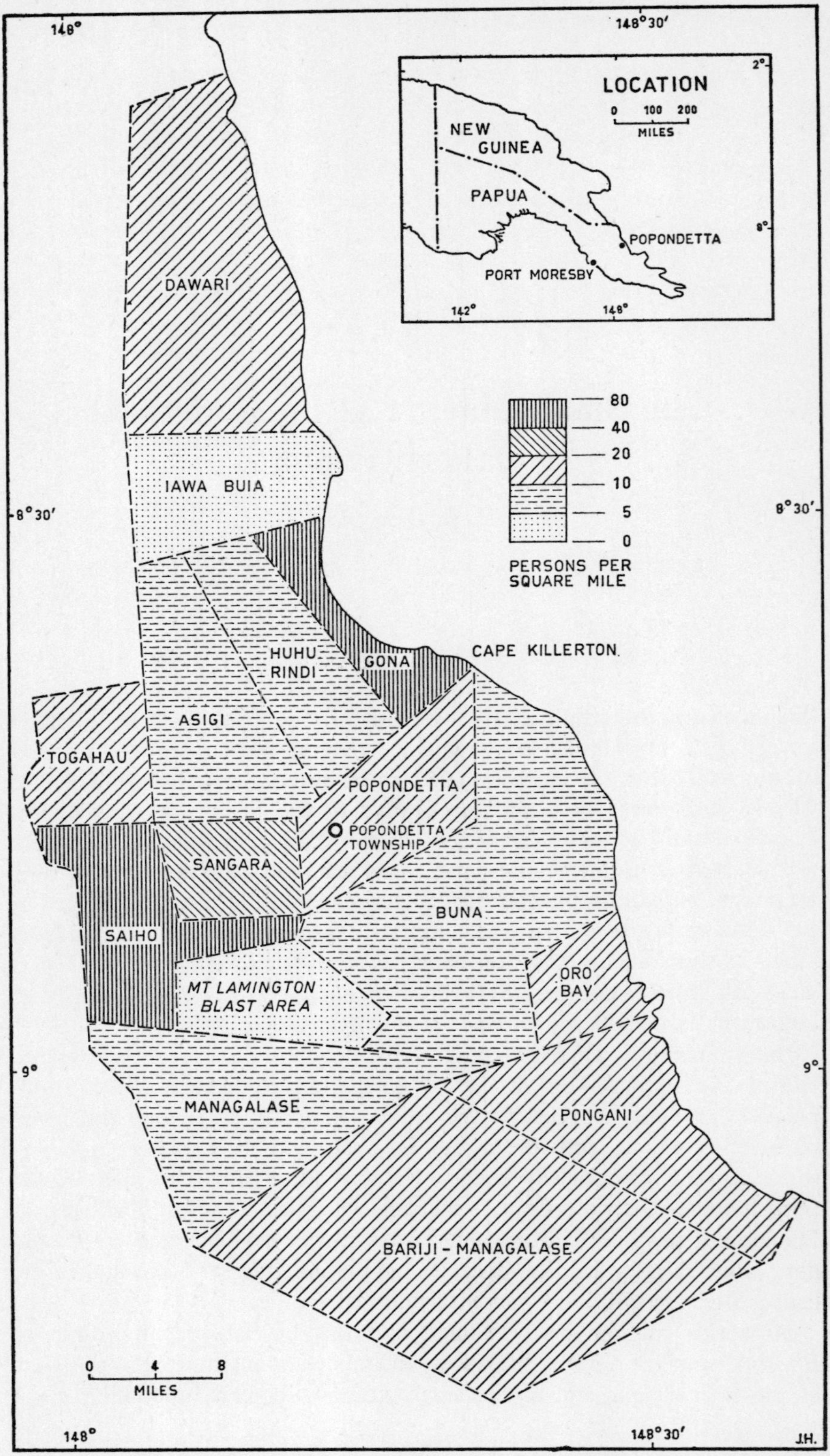

Map 2 *Popondetta Sub-district, Papua, showing density of population*

does as a source of fresh food for the town-dwellers and as an outlet for surplus produce and a source of cash income for the villagers.[1]

Popondetta market is the principal of three commercial outlets for the surplus garden produce of the indigenes living within a twenty-mile radius of Popondetta township. The other two outlets are the Administration Hospital at Saiho and the Anglican Mission T.B. Hospital at Embogo, both of which purchase large quantities of locally grown vegetables. There are, however, very many people living in Popondetta Sub-district and many whose homes are within twenty miles of Popondetta who seldom attend the market. On the other hand, almost every market day there may be found one or two people who have come very long distances to sell relatively high-priced commodities such as pigmeat, *tapa* cloth, or pottery with some special aim in view, such as the payment of tax or bride-price.

The original market-place was a small area of cleared land about fifty yards square on the northern outskirts of the township. On this site was built an open-sided, thatched shed about fifteen feet by forty feet; inside the shed and on the open space around were erected low tables of bush poles on which sellers displayed their wares. By mid-1964 the site had become so overcrowded that fully one-third of all sellers had to display their produce on the ground. The use of this site was discontinued in July 1964, when a new site, much more spacious, and with a large concrete-floored, tin-roofed shelter shed, was opened about 300 yards northwest of the old site. The market starts at daybreak on Saturday mornings and usually trading has ceased by about 10.30 a.m. Entry to the old market was free, but sellers pay a 5 cent fee to use the new market. Money collected in this way is a source of revenue for the Oro Bay Local Government Council.

Between 1963 and 1964 there was a marked increase in the proportion of buyers coming from outside the town area. The data are summarised in Table II. 1. In the 1963 sample, 77 per cent of buyers were 'migrants' from outside Popondetta Sub-district. In 1964 this proportion had dropped to 59 per cent. Many more settlers from the nearby resettlement blocks at Sangara and Isivita were attending the market in 1964 than in 1963. This seems to indicate an increasing buying power on the part of this group.

Almost all Papuan buyers walked to market. Of those living outside the town most walked in, several received free lifts, one owned his own motor cycle, and two came by pedal cycle. All Europeans, whether

[1]The research data on which this paper is based were collected in six surveys on 1 and 15 December 1962, 19 January and 2 February 1963, and 11 and 18 July 1964. The first four surveys were conducted by the author and two field assistants. Twenty students of the Popondetta Agricultural Training Institute assisted with the 1964 surveys. All surveys were made as part of a wider study of the Yega people living in Gona census division (Dakeyne 1965).

Table II. 1 Place of residence of buyers in Popondetta market, January 1963 and July 1964

Place of residence	January 1963 (group of 60) (No.)	(%)	July 1964 (group of 204) (No.)	(%)
Popondetta township	41	68	99	48
Sawmill and agricultural station	4	7	9	4
Papuan and New Guinean settlers, Sangara	1	2	15	7
Villages within 5 miles radius of Popondetta*	4	7	45	22
Villages more than 5 miles from Popondetta*	10	17	36	18

*Most of these buyers are sellers who, having sold their own produce, purchase other goods such as meat, fish, betel nut, or betel pepper to take home. Most of the Papuan and New Guinean residents of Popondetta stated that they depended almost entirely on the market for regular supplies of fresh food.

living in the town or outside it, came by motor vehicle.

When I first visited the market early in 1963 I saw only a small number of European buyers; in addition, a few Europeans sent their Papuan or New Guinean servants to buy fruit and vegetables. I estimated at that time that spending by Europeans accounted for less than 5 per cent of the weekly market turnover. During 1963 and early 1964 there was a big increase in the European population of Popondetta, and by July 1964 the number of European buyers had at least tripled since January 1963. However, there had been little apparent attempt on the part of Papuan suppliers to meet the increased demand of Europeans for special produce such as tomatoes, pineapples, and fresh vegetables. This was a source of complaint among European buyers.

The supply of the market

The road network is a factor of major importance in determining the sphere of influence of the market. This does not imply that most sellers come to market by motor vehicle; in fact, almost all walk to market, except a few who travel by truck or in the Higaturu Council trailer. The normal fare charged is 20 cents or 30 cents, depending upon the distance travelled. Other people living at Cape Killerton or along the Popondetta-Cape Killerton road are sometimes given free lifts in private trucks. Most of the people who travel this way are Yega from Surilai and Niniyanda villages, or Bapa, Andere, and Kuroro people from Garara village. Means of travel to market by sellers is summarised in Table II. 2.

Table II. 2 Sellers in Popondetta market – means of travel to market (sample group of 40 sellers), January 1963

Means of travel	Number	Percentage
Walked entire distance	32	80
Motor transport – paid fare	1	2·5
Motor transport – did not pay fare	4	10
Coastal vessel – paid fare; walked from coast	2	5
Canoe – walked from coast	1	2·5

The sphere of influence of the market is shown on Map 3. On this map are shown the road network, the names, and approximate locations (not all could be found on the available maps) of villages from which at least one member attended the market on the days on which surveys were made.

In order to assist sellers who live long distances from Popondetta, a large thatched sleeping platform was built at the roadside, fifty yards from the old market area. This platform accommodates fifty to sixty

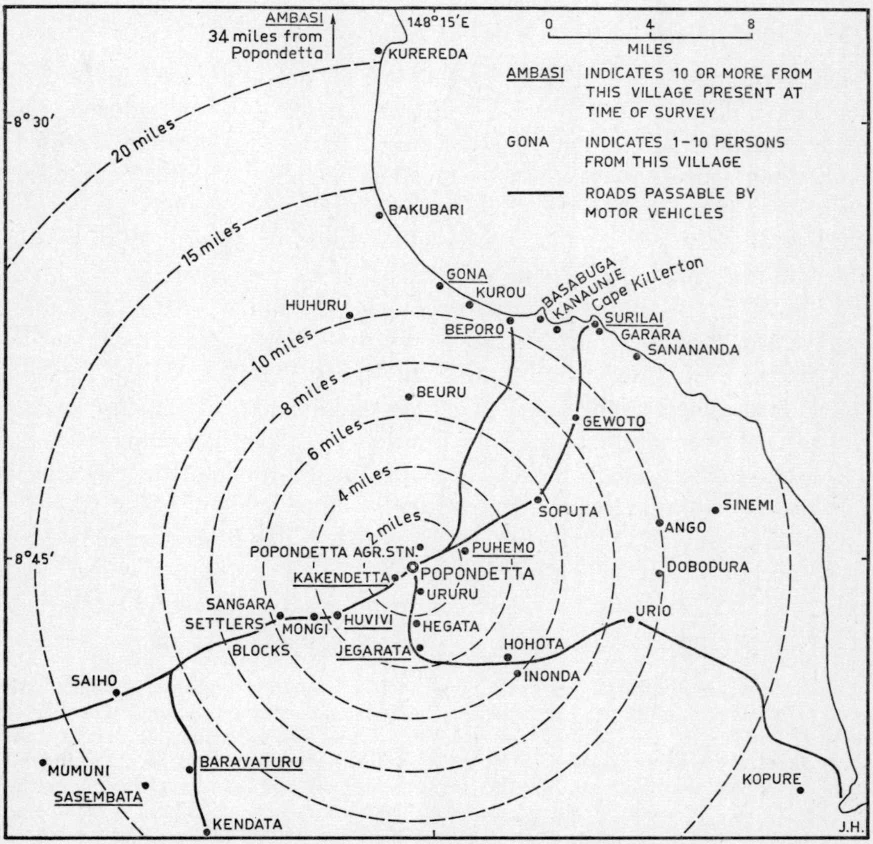

Map 3 *Distribution of villages supplying Popondetta market, Papua*

people, and by nightfall on Friday evenings all available places have been taken. Most sellers who live more than five miles out walk in to Popondetta on Friday mornings and spend the day visiting friends or looking round the trade stores. They then sleep on the platform and arrive early at the market on Saturday to obtain good positions.

Sellers usually operate in groups of related kin which I shall call family groups. A characteristic group might include a man, his wife, their two teen-age daughters and one of his brother's daughters. These groups are predominantly female, thus most sellers are women. However, men do sell in the market, and appear to concentrate on such lines as betel nut, meat, and fish. The family group system results in a large number of people standing about at the backs of the stalls, giving the impression of many sellers, each having a very small amount of produce on sale. This impression is strengthened by the fact that any member of the family group may apparently quote a price for an item when asked by a prospective buyer; she may also accept payment.

Trade in the market

Most transactions are in cash, and almost all goods are sold in 10 cent lots, or multiples of 10 cents.[2] Prices cannot thus be reduced, but sometimes late in the morning the size of a 10 cent heap is doubled, and when European produce is in short supply but strong demand, quantities may be halved; thus a 10 cent 'heap' of tomatoes might consist of only two tomatoes instead of four, or three. With goods that can be sold only in single units, such as watermelons and pineapples, even this limited measure of price flexibility is not available. In general, this does not seem to worry the sellers, who are content to sustain an even price at all times. In Rabaul market, where Epstein (1961) encountered the same phenomenon, the web of kinship among matrilineal people may be a factor inhibiting competition among sellers. It seems unlikely that this is a major factor among the patrilineal Orokaiva, who are strongly competitive in other fields of activity.

Total turnover is small, but, as Table II. 3 demonstrates, it is very unbalanced: about half the total produce sold consists of betel nut, tobacco, fish, and meat, goods commanding a relatively high price. This is perhaps to be related to the wide catchment of so small a

[2]There is a little barter, and during school term a large volume of fresh fruit and vegetables is obtained by pupils of Popondetta Secondary School, who barter salt (provided by the school) for produce. Some sellers refuse to accept salt, but others are willing to do so, and the children have no trouble in obtaining all the vegetables they require. In this way the school obtains cheap food and the sellers dispose of produce that might otherwise remain unsold. There is also some bartering of unsold produce among sellers near the end of the trading period or when other buyers have left the market (see Table II.4).

market, for most of these goods are brought from a distance. Demand for staple foods is clearly either limited, or else not satisfied.

Trading is affected by the fortnightly schedule of Administration pay-days, turnover being about 20 per cent less on the intervening weeks. Though it was not possible to check all sales, since some goods are in great demand and are sold very quickly, surveys suggest that on the pay-day weekends turnover was between $140 and $160. In July 1964, turnover at a 'pay-day' market reached $142, but at a 'non-pay-day' market only $112.

The main purpose of my research was, as indicated above, to understand the contribution of market trading to the economy of the Yega

Table II. 3 Popondetta market – value of produce sold on two market days in January and February 1963, by produce classes

Item	Market days 19/1/63 ($)	2/2/63 ($)	Average ($)	Percentage
Sago	1.30	1.10	1.20	0·8
Taro	12.00	7.50	9.70	6·4
Sweet Potatoes	6.80	3.00	4.90	4·5
Coconuts	6.80	14.30	10.50	7·0
Bananas	9.30	6.50	7.90	5·2
Other fruit	8.40	3.30	5.80	3·8
Betel nut and tobacco	50.40	33.10	41.70	27·7
Fish and meat	36.70	34.60	35.50	23·4
All other produce	17.90	41.90	29.90	19·7
Total	157.60	145.30	151.40	98·5

Note: In addition to minor agricultural produce such as beans and *pitpit*, the 'all other produce' category includes high value items such as pots, mats, *tapa* cloth, bread rolls, ready-made dresses and skirts, lime pots, and string bags.

Taro and sweet potatoes are plentiful in January, so the demand for sago is small. Informants stated that much larger quantities of sago appear in the market around July-August.

people, and I have more detailed information on the Yega sellers. Yega make up only a small proportion of the sellers in the market, probably about 4 per cent of selling groups in 1963, but rather more in 1964, when as many as fifteen of seventy or eighty family groups in the market were Yega. None the less, the Yega offer a full range of produce, and their activities are in many ways representative. Data presented in Tables II. 4 and II. 5 indicate wide variation in dependence on the market as a source of income. The fourteen Yega families represented are drawn from over a hundred families in the Yega group, and in 1963 the total cash income accruing to all Yega from market sources was less than $10 per week. By 1964 the total Yega cash income from this source had undoubtedly increased, but it is still true to say that for most families only a negligible amount of money is earned in this way. On the other hand a very few families – some four or five – earn regularly from $1 to $2.50 per week.

Irregularity of market attendance is characteristic of all groups, including the Yega. In each village there appears to be a small nucleus of families who depend heavily on the market for their cash earnings, but most families sell produce only when they need the money to buy some specific item, or to pay tax. Popondetta market has not yet reached a stage at which the rural-dwelling indigenes depend heavily on it for income, but it is essential to the town-dwellers, most of whom

Table II. 4 Sale of produce and disposal of unsold produce by 14 Yega villagers on three visits to Popondetta market in December 1962, January and February 1963

Family group No.	Total value of produce taken to market ($)	Value of goods sold ($)	Disposal of unsold produce
1	2.40	1.60	All taken home
2	2.40	0.60	Lime exchanged for taro, remainder taken home
3	2.00	0.50	All taken home
4	1.40	0.90	All taken home
5	2.00	1.80	All taken home
6	1.00	0.60	Fish exchanged for taro, remainder taken home
7	1.80	1.60	All taken home
8	0.40	0.40	—
9	1.30	0.90	All taken home
10	1.30	1.00	Bananas eaten, remainder taken home
11	3.20	1.50	Lime exchanged for betel nut, remainder taken home
12	1.80	1.00	All taken home
13	2.50	2.50	—
14	6.20	5.10	Green coconuts eaten, remainder taken home
Averages	2.12	1.43	

are migrants to the area, and who would have to buy more expensive canned and processed food were the market not in existence. There are certainly opportunities for expansion, especially in the supply of vegetables in demand by Europeans, such as tomatoes, beans, lettuce, potatoes, and maize, all of which grow well on the higher slopes of Mt Lamington quite close to Popondetta.

Table II. 5 Sale of produce, disposal of unsold produce, and disposal of profits among a sample group of Yega sellers at Popondetta market on 19 and 26 January 1963

Informant	Produce taken to market	Price asked ($)	Produce sold	Sum obtained ($)	Produce unsold	Disposal of unsold produce	Disposal of profits	Regularity of visits to market
19 January 1963								
A	2 taro	0.10	all	0.10			shared with	
(wife)	4 sweet potatoes	0.10	all	0.10		—	husband, bought	
	1 pawpaw	0.10	all	0.10	nil		tinned meat and	bi-monthly
	1 pkt lime	0.10	all	0.10			some sugar	
	Total	0.40		0.40				
B	2 taro	0.10	all	0.10	—		shared with	weekly
(husband	4 sweet potatoes	0.10	all	0.10	—		wife, part for	(sick last
and wife)	4 coconuts	0.20	all	0.20	—	taken	mission	two weeks)
	3 pineapples	0.60	one	0.20	2	home	offertory	
	1 pkt lime	0.10	all	0.10	—			
	2 fish	0.20	all	0.20	—			
	Total	1.30		0.90				
C	4 taro	0.20	all	0.20	—		shared with	
(wife)	8 sweet potatoes	0.20	all	0.20	—		husband,	
	6 coconuts	0.30	2	0.10	4	taken	bought	weekly
	hand bananas	0.10	n.s.	—	all	home	biscuits, meat	
	3 pkts lime	0.30	all	0.30	—		and sugar with	
	2 fish	0.20	all	0.20	—		part	
	Total	1.30		1.00				

(continued on next page)

Table II. 5 *(continued)*

Informant	Produce taken to market	Price asked ($)	Produce sold	Sum obtained ($)	Produce unsold	Disposal of unsold produce	Disposal of profits	Regularity of visits to market
26 January 1963								
D	4 coconuts	0.20	2	0.10	2	1 pkt lime	spent 70c on	
(wife)	24 limes	0.20	all	0.20	—	bartered for	a towel, rice	
	4 crabs	0.40	2	0.20	2	12 betel nuts,	and tobacco,	
	2 baskets shellfish	2.00	1 basket	1.00	1	remainder	remainder	monthly
	4 pkts lime	0.40	n.s.	—	4	taken home	saved for	
	Total	3.20		1.50			skirt for daughter	
E	4 coconuts	0.20	n.s.	—	4		spent 10c on betel	
(wife)	4 pkts lime	0.40	all	0.40	—		nut at market, and	monthly
	28 small fish	0.60	24	0.60	4	taken home	60c on tinned fish	
	1 mat	0.60	n.s.	—	1		and biscuits at store	
	Total	1.80		1.00				
F	1 leg pork	1.50	all	1.50	—	—		
(wife and	2 pieces pork						not stated	irregular
daughter)	(smoked)	1.00	all	1.00	—	—		
	Total	2.50		2.50				
G	4 lime pots	2.00	all	2.00	—	4 green	money shared	
(husband,	4 coconuts	0.20	all	0.20	—	coconuts	out,	
wife, and	4 pkts sago	0.40	3	0.30	1	used	wife $1,	
2 daughters)	3 mats	1.50	2	1.00	1	for food,	2 daughters	
	3 pawpaw	0.30	n.s.	—	3	all remainder	50c each	weekly
	4 green coconuts	0.20	n.s.	—	4	taken home		
	2 smoked fish	0.40	all	0.40	—			
	4 crabs	0.80	all	0.80	—			
	12 taro	0.40	all	0.40	—			
	Total	6.20		5.10				

n.s. = no sale.

III

Supplies and Prices in the Market at Kerema, Gulf District, Papua

G. R. Hogbin

Kerema, the administrative centre of the Gulf District of Papua, is a settlement of approximately 500 Papuans, New Guineans, and expatriates, almost all of whom are government employees or their dependants. It lies in a region which, although subjected to governmental and missionary influences for over sixty years, has a poorly developed cash economy and few modern transport facilities. However, some local people, especially those from villages on the coast, have acquired wider experience of the cash economy by working in towns and on plantations outside the District. The slow development of the cash economy is reflected by the fact that although the government station at Kerema was established in 1906, in 1963 there was still only one small retail store in the town area, plus a co-operative store in a nearby Papuan village. Until a market-place was established in 1961, people wishing to buy fresh, locally produced foods in Kerema were forced to rely on hawkers or some other informal source of supply.

Because of the background of limited economic development, the market was the first institution in the area to draw local Papuans together in some sort of competitive situation within the cash economy and in a setting in which cash was the sole means of exchange. In 1963, in the course of a field study of the nearby Cupisi rubber project

Most of the preparation of this paper was done while the author was a Research Assistant in the Economics Department, Research School of Pacific Studies, Australian National University. He acknowledges with gratitude the help given by Mr E. K. Fisk and by Drs H. C. Brookfield and R. G. Crocombe.

(G. R. Hogbin 1964) I conducted a brief survey of the market. Initially I was interested in the extent to which the three villages involved in the rubber project (Karaeta, Siviri, and Uriri) made use of it, but as the survey progressed it proved possible to widen the scope of the study. In particular, an effort was made to assess the part which the market plays in the indigenous sector of the Kerema Bay cash economy and to isolate some of the principles of economic behaviour of buyers and sellers in the market.

Location of the market

Kerema is situated about 150 miles west of Port Moresby near the entrance of Kerema Bay, the common mouth of a system of rivers flowing into the Gulf of Papua (Map 4). The market is located in pleasant surroundings in the Kerema administration station area, on high ground overlooking the bay. Most of the market produce is

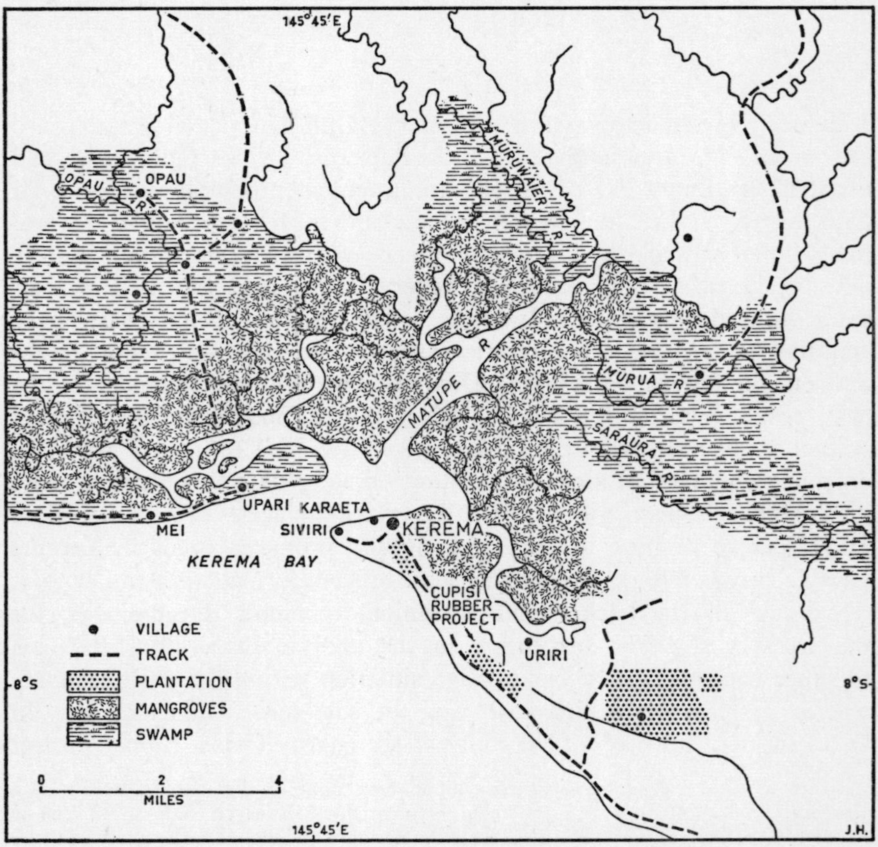

Map 4 *Distribution of villages supplying Kerema market, Papua*

brought to Kerema by canoe and carried from the shore of the bay to the market-place, a distance of about a quarter of a mile. A road suitable for motor vehicles runs past the market-place and connects with the limited road system in the station area, but this was little used at the time of the survey. The only produce transported by motor vehicle was that bought by the Administration.

In 1961, a Papuan contracted with the Administration to build a galvanised-iron roofed market building using bush timber supplied by local village people. Display benches about four feet from the ground were constructed along the sides and down the middle of the building, which was thirty feet by twenty feet. On the main market days there is usually insufficient bench space to display all produce and consequently some is placed on the grass surrounding the building. A spring balance hangs in one corner of the building, but the only produce weighed is that bought by the Administration.

Survey techniques

The market at Kerema is much smaller than those in larger towns in Papua-New Guinea and it was possible to record details of all produce brought and sold. The data were collected by two Papuan assistants who were fluent in the local language, Tairuma, but not in the language of some inland villages from which produce came. The assistants reported that, in general, vendors and buyers co-operated willingly in the survey.

As each vendor brought his produce to the market, a survey assistant noted his name, the village from which he came, the quantities of goods brought, and the time at which he arrived at the market. Similarly, when a buyer made a purchase his name, his place of residence, the quantity of produce bought, the amount paid, and the time at which the purchase was made were recorded. When all buying had ceased a record of the quantities of produce remaining unsold was taken.[1] The assistants did not have sufficient time to weigh the produce as it arrived, so it was quantified in the units in which it was brought to the market. For example, sago was counted by bundles, and taro, sweet potato, and corn by baskets. During the survey, samples of the unit in which a particular type of produce was most frequently sold were weighed in order to obtain an indication of the average weight of the unit. It was difficult to assess the weight of items such as fish, shellfish, crabs, and certain fruits, because both the weights of these and the sizes of the lots into which they were grouped for sale varied greatly.

[1]Except for the first two days of the survey.

Marketing procedure

Although the market functioned on three or four days of the week, the turnover of produce was usually much greater on Mondays than on other days (Tables III. 1 and III. 2), mainly because Administration departments bought most of their market food requirements at that time. There was, however, no regular schedule of market days.

Usually some vendors arrived at the market about 7 a.m., most had arrived by about 9 a.m., but some came as late as 11 a.m. Buying started soon after the first produce arrived and continued until about noon, provided that all produce had not been sold before that time. On one day during the survey there was a total clearance of supplies, but on most days a small amount of produce remained unsold. The only day of the survey when a large quantity remained unsold was 11 March (Table III. 3). It is not known whether vendors took their surplus produce home, whether they offered it for sale on the following day, or whether they disposed of it by some other means before returning home.

Table III. 1 Quantities of produce brought to Kerema market over a two-week period, 25 February to 10 March 1963

Produce	Week 1						Week 2			
	Mon.	Wed.	Thu.	Fri.	Sat.	Total	Mon.	Thu.	Fri.	Total
Sago (bundles approx. av. weight 35 lb)	16					16	50	5		55
Taro (baskets approx. av. weight 33 lb)	37	2	6		12	57	47	9	6	62
Sweet potatoes (baskets approx. av. weight 30 lb)	3	4	½	1	1	9½		2	2	4
Corn (baskets approx. av. weight 10 lb)	1		1	1		3	1	4		5
Breadfruit	1			6	4	11		3		3
Cabbage and *pitpit* (bundles usually worth 20c)	8		2		2	12		8		8
Sugar cane (bundles)								6		6
Bananas (bunch approx. av. weight 17 lb)	31	15	2		2	50	49	8	41	98
Melons	15			8		23	22	5	5	32
Pineapples	27	8	2		3	40	12	4		16
Oranges (lots of 4 to 8)					1	1	2	1		3
Other fruit (usually sold in lots worth 10c to 20c)	5					5				
Fish (large fish = 2, small fish = 1)	12		14	8	4	38	8	2		10
Shellfish (baskets) and crabs (lots of 3 to 5)	14				5	19	18	19	6	43
Eggs	13					13				
Pig-meat (portion)							1			1
Betel nuts (basket or bunch)	6	2	4	11	11	34	3	14	3	20
Pepper (bundle)			3	9		12		8		8
Bread (loaves)	6					6		21		21

Table III. 2 Quantities of produce brought to Kerema market on Mondays 25 February to 8 April 1963

Produce	25/2/63	4/3/63	11/3/63	18/3/63	8/4/63
Sago (bundles approx. av. weight 35 lb)	16	50	31	19	36
Taro (baskets approx. av. weight 33 lb)	37	47	49	55	53
Sweet potatoes (baskets approx. av. weight 30 lb)	3		9	3	4
Corn (baskets approx. av. weight 10 lb)	1	1	2	1	
Breadfruit	1		4		
Cabbage and *pitpit* (bundles usually worth 20c)	8		10	2	2
Sugar cane (bundles)				3	
Bananas (bunches approx. av. weight 17 lb)	31	49	5	23	26
Melons	15	22	5	17	16
Pineapples	27	12	12	4	12
Oranges (lots of 4 to 8)		2	4	2	
Other fruit (usually sold in lots worth 10c to 20c)	5		3	3	
Fish (large fish = 2, small fish = 1)	12	8	2	3	13
Shellfish (baskets) and crabs (lots of 3 to 5)	14	18	3	7	15
Eggs	13		2		
Pig-meat (portion)		1			
Betel nuts (basket or bunch)	6	3	9	13	5
Pepper (bundle)			2	11	5
Bread (loaves)	6		39		22

Table III. 3 Quantities of produce remaining unsold at Kerema market on certain days from 28 February to 8 April 1963

Produce	Thu. 28 Feb.	Fri. 1 Mar.	Sat. 2 Mar.	Mon. 4 Mar.	Thu. 7 Mar.	Fri. 8 Mar.	Mon. 11 Mar.	Mon. 18 Mar.	Mon. 8 Apr.
Sago (bundles)							4		
Taro (baskets)	2		1	5	1	3	26		
Sweet potatoes (baskets)									
Corn (baskets)		1			1				
Breadfruit		6							
Cabbage and *pitpit* (bundles)					4		2		
Sugar cane (bundles)									
Bananas (bunches)	1				2	2			
Melons		7		5					10
Pineapples									9
Oranges (baskets)							2		
Other fruit (lots)						1			
Fish	1								10
Shellfish (baskets) and crabs (lots)						3	2		7
Eggs									
Pig-meat									
Betel nuts	1	4	1	1	1	2	4		
Pepper	1	1			1				

Supply areas

Almost all of the produce brought to the market came from villages situated within ten miles of Kerema station. The two main supply areas were the area west of Kerema station across Kerema Bay, including the coastal or near-coastal villages of Mei, Uaripi, and Opau, and the area further inland from Kerema through which the rivers entering Kerema Bay run. The people from the former area are almost entirely Elema people.[2] Those from the latter area are predominantly inland tribesmen, though some Elema people live there. The people living in the villages close to Kerema station and to the east brought relatively little produce to the market. Excluding the population of the township of Kerema, it is estimated that about 3,000 people were living in these supply areas, but only a small proportion of these villagers sold produce regularly at the market. The size of the supply area was possibly limited by the high labour cost of transporting the produce in relation to the value of sales which a vendor could expect to make. Rivers and beaches provide the only access routes to Kerema and in 1963 paddle canoes were the only universally available vehicles for transporting the produce. The labour cost of bringing produce from villages outside the existing supply areas would have been high.

Table III. 4 shows that during the survey the coastal and near-coastal villages supplied all the sago and the bulk of the fish, shellfish, melons, betel nut, and pepper.[3] Other important products from these areas were taro and bananas. In contrast, the inland villages supplied the bulk of the taro and bananas, but no sago. Other major items from the inland areas were pineapples, sweet potato, betel nut, and various leafy vegetables which local people refer to collectively as 'cabbage'. Two men who had small-scale bakeries in Siviri and Karaeta sold bread, but apart from that, the people from the villages associated with the Cupisi project sold very little produce at the market. Although the total number of people resident in Karaeta, Siviri, and Uriri was over 950, only 18 sold produce during the survey.

Table III. 5 shows both the value of the sales made at the market and the number of vendors who brought produce to the market for each day of the survey. The cash income received by a vendor for his sales averaged $1.39 per day and did not vary significantly with the supply area from which he came.

[2]The indigenous people occupying the coastal areas fringing the Gulf of Papua between Cape Possession in the east and the Purari delta in the west constitute one ethnic group which has become known as the 'Elema' (Williams 1940:23-5).

[3]The term 'pepper' will be used in this paper to describe the various plant materials chewed with betel nut.

Table III. 4 Quantities of produce brought to Kerema market from different parts of the supply area on the days during which the survey was conducted

Produce	Karaeta, Siviri, Uriri*	Mei, Uaripi, Opau†	Inland villages
Sago (bundles approx. av. weight 35 lb)	16	141	
Taro (baskets approx. av. weight 33 lb)		70	199
Sweet potatoes (baskets approx. av. weight 30 lb)		5½	24
Corn (baskets approx. av. weight 10 lb)		7	4
Breadfruit	1	13	4
Cabbage and *pitpit* (bundles usually worth 20c)		15	19
Bananas (bundles approx. av. weight 17 lb)		39	163
Melons	2	85	2
Pineapples		9	75
Oranges (lots of 4 to 8)		10	
Other fruit (usually sold in lots worth 10c or 20c)	3	10	3
Fish (large fish = 2, small fish = 1)	8	56	2
Shellfish (baskets) and crabs (lots of 3 to 5)	6	71	10
Eggs		10	5
Pig-meat (portion)		1	
Betel nuts (basket or bunch)	4	61	16
Pepper (bundle)	2	34	2
Bread (loaves)	88		

*Villages associated with the Cupisi rubber project.

†Other coastal villages or near-coastal villages, predominantly those west of Kerema.

Table III. 5 Value of sales by vendors from different parts of the supply area of Kerema market on certain dates. Number of vendors shown in parentheses

Date	Karaeta, Siviri, Uriri ($)	Mei, Uaripi, Opau ($)	Inland villages ($)	Total ($)
Mon. 25 Feb.	3.10 (4)	35.30 (13)	19.90 (19)	58.30 (36)
Tue. 26 Feb.				
Wed. 27 Feb.		0.20 (1)	14.10 (6)	14.30 (7)
Thur. 28 Feb.		7.20 (6)		7.20 (6)
Fri. 1 Mar.		2.95 (15)		2.95 (15)
Sat. 2 Mar.	n.s. (1)	3.85 (7)	0.95 (11)	4.80 (19)
Total (week)	3.10 (5)	49.50 (42)	34.95 (36)	87.55 (83)
Mon. 4 Mar.	0.60 (1)	38.54 (22)	15.80 (21)	54.94 (44)
Tue. 5 Mar.				
Wed. 6 Mar.				
Thur. 7 Mar.	3.80 (2)	14.25 (24)	3.15 (4)	21.20 (30)
Fri. 8 Mar.		8.65 (16)	2.00 (2)	10.65 (18)
Sat. 9 Mar.				
Total (week)	4.40 (3)	61.44 (62)	20.95 (27)	86.79 (92)
Mon. 11 Mar.	8.15 (8)	35.27 (27)	19.92 (18)	63.34 (53)
Mon. 18 Mar.	0.20 (1)	47.95 (21)	16.92 (11)	65.07 (33)
Mon. 8 Apr.	13.83 (6)	54.74 (12)	26.42 (9)	94.99 (27)

n.s. = no sale.

The buying forces

Table III. 6 shows that during the days of the survey, the Administration bought food worth about $200, and that it constituted the main buying force. Just under 70 per cent of the other buyers were people employed by the Administration and in other occupations at Kerema, or dependants of these people. In the course of a week, this group of buyers spent at the market approximately the same amount of money as the Administration. The remainder of the purchases was made by people from Siviri and Karaeta and from other more distant villages, but in total, village people bought only about $20 worth of produce during the survey and accounted for only a small proportion of the buying force.

Table III. 6 Value of purchases made in Kerema market by four classes of buyers on certain dates. Number of buyers shown in parentheses.

Date	Administration ($)	Administration employees and others at Kerema station ($)	Siviri, Karaeta, and Uriri villagers ($)	Other buyers ($)	Total ($)
Mon. 25 Feb.	?	?	?	?	58.30
Tue. 26 Feb.					
Wed. 27 Feb.	?	?			14.30
Thur. 28 Feb.	4.60	2.15 (7)		0.50 (1)	7.25
Fri. 1 Mar.		2.95 (4)			2.95
Sat. 2 Mar.		4.40 (12)	0.40 (1)		4.80
Total (week)					87.60
Mon. 4 Mar.	39.59	14.15 (21)	1.00 (1)	0.20 (1)	54.94
Tue. 5 Mar.					
Wed. 6 Mar.					
Thur. 7 Mar.		15.40 (17)	0.70 (2)	5.10 (13)	21.20
Fri. 8 Mar.	4.60	4.50 (12)	0.35 (2)	1.20 (5)	10.65
Sat. 9 Mar.					
Total (week)	44.19	34.05 (50)	2.05 (5)	6.50 (19)	46.79
Mon. 11 Mar.	26.79	25.96 (38)	6.60 (10)	3.00 (14)	62.35
Mon. 18 Mar.	40.42	22.00 (21)	1.80 (5)	0.65 (2)	64.87
Mon. 8 Apr.	40.80	49.40 (27)		4.80 (13)	95.00

It is clear that one of the reasons for the low volume of sales was the comparatively small number of people who wished to buy goods in the market. It is reasonable to assume that people living in the townships provide the main buying forces at markets in Papua-New Guinea. In Kerema, where the population of town-dwellers is only about 500, the demand for market goods is small compared with the demand in larger towns in the Territory.

The place of the market in the Kerema Bay economy

Between 1 April 1961 and 31 March 1962 the value of recorded primary production in the indigenous sector of the cash economy of the Kerema Bay census division was just over $12,000.[4] If supplies and prices were maintained at the levels which prevailed at the time of the survey it is likely that the turnover at the Kerema market during 1963 would have been between $4,000 and $5,000, so that it is clear that the market has become established as an important part of the Kerema Bay cash economy. As there does not appear to be any reason why supplies could not be increased, future expansion of the market will probably depend on increases in demand. For this reason possibilities of increasing demand for market produce are worth examining.

A survey of the expenditure patterns of four groups of people from Siviri, Karaeta, and Uriri villages showed that of the total cash spent on food, 56 per cent was used to buy imported carbohydrate foods such as sugar, rice, flour, bread, and biscuits (35 per cent for sugar, rice, and flour) while only 12 per cent was used to buy local carbohydrate foods (G. R. Hogbin 1964: Ch. 4). In terms of the number of calories which could be bought per unit of expenditure, sago, taro, cooking bananas, and possibly sweet potatoes were considerably cheaper than sugar, rice, flour, bread, and biscuits (Table III. 7). If this fact were used as a basis for promoting the buying of market foods, it is possible that the demand for such foods could be increased. The Kerema Bay Local Government Council and local women's clubs could provide the focal points for a promotion campaign. Some people from local villages said they were reluctant to buy at the market because they feared that others would cast aspersions on their abilities as gardeners. If these fears were important inhibiting factors, they will probably be overcome when people become more accustomed to the market.

Table III. 7 Number of calories which could be purchased in Kerema market for 10 cents for the main carbohydrate foods available in 1963*

Market		Co-operative and trade stores	
Foods	Calories	Foods	Calories
Sago	6,020	Flour	2,100
Taro	3,010	Sugar	1,820
Bananas	2,560	White rice	1,580

*The calorific values of these foods have been taken from Platt (1945). Platt also gives, for each type of food, a figure for the percentage (by weight) of food bought which is wasted in preparing it for cooking. Allowances for such wastage have been taken into account in the figures presented in this table.

[4]District Commissioner's Annual Report, Gulf District, Papua (Department of Agriculture, Kerema, File 43-6-B).

It may be possible for the Administration to increase turnover at the market by insisting that its departments use local fresh foods instead of equivalent imported foods for rations, except when supplies of local foods are inadequate. Although there are problems in handling the local foods, the advantages to the local economy should outweigh the difficulties which might be encountered. The possibility of marketing locally grown foods at Port Moresby could also be examined, but high freight rates (approximately 3 cents per pound in 1963) and additional undetermined handling costs may make this an uneconomic proposition.

Pricing

On arrival at the market, a vendor would select a suitable place to heap his produce and then stand or sit beside it waiting patiently for a buyer. There was no set place in the market for vendors from a particular village. In contrast to the Rabaul market, where most of the vendors were women, approximately equal numbers of men and women sold produce at Kerema. Also, all transactions were made with cash. In the Rabaul market roughly 10 per cent of transactions were made with shell money, the traditional medium of exchange (Epstein 1961). It was difficult to determine the time at which the vendors at Kerema fixed the price on their produce, but they had no difficulty in specifying prices almost immediately on arrival at the market. Vendors made no positive attempt to advertise their products and adopted a 'take-it-or-leave-it' attitude similar to attitudes which Epstein describes for Rabaul market. A clear characteristic of the Kerema market was the absence of competition between buyers. Epstein (1961: 53) contrasts the behaviour of the vendors in Rabaul market with that in markets in other parts of the world.

> At Rabaul market the prospective buyer can walk around examining the goods offered by as many sellers as he wishes without being invited to buy by any of them, while in India or Camden town, anyone walking through the market is solicited by each and every seller who tries to impress on the buyer that his goods are far better than any other's in the market.

The reason for the difference in the behaviour of vendors in Papua-New Guinea compared with vendors in other parts of the world might perhaps lie in the difference in extent of commitment to the cash economy. In Papua-New Guinea, where the vast majority of vendors are still basically dependent on the subsistence economy and subsistence activities for their material wants, the need for cash is not fundamental to existence. Where it is essential for a vendor to acquire cash in order to obtain his material requirements for living, his anxiety to make a sale will be very much greater. He will be forced into a highly competitive situation and to adopt techniques of selling which increase a buyer's willingness to buy. In other words, the behaviour of the vendors in markets in Papua-New Guinea suggests that they place a low value on cash compared with vendors in most other parts of the world.

There was little evidence of bargaining between Papuan buyers and sellers. The sellers, who appeared to pay little if any attention to prospective buyers until it became obvious that a sale was almost certain to be made, did not seem to be at all upset if potential buyers decided not to buy. On the other hand an expatriate buyer could, with a minimum of bargaining, quite frequently reduce the price of an item, especially if it was over-priced in relation to similar items available elsewhere in the market. There was, however, a minimum price which the vendor was prepared to accept and if the expatriate tried to get a lower price, the vendor would soon lose all interest in the sale, making little or no attempt to persuade the buyer to pay the minimum price.

There seemed to be two clear characteristics of the price-forming mechanism. On the one hand, vendors appeared to be making positive attempts to price their produce within rigid limits and to be almost unaware of the part which the market forces of supply and demand may play in determining prices. On the other hand, prices for what were apparently similar products were in fact extremely variable, principally because of an inability on the part of almost all vendors and many of the buyers to assess weights accurately and to use small units of currency precisely and efficiently. However, it is likely that prices would appear to be rigid to the majority of the people of the market.

A vendor has at his disposal two methods of consciously valuing produce according to weight. First, he may assess the weight of the item and then decide on the price. Village people show an obvious distaste for dealing in small units of currency; transactions are seldom made in change smaller than 5 cents and the great majority of produce is sold in lots valued at 10 cents or multiples of 10 cents. This first method leads to wide variations in price. For example, although small baskets of taro usually sold for 10 cents, medium-weight baskets for 20 cents, and large baskets for 30 cents, sellers in different parts of the market might be asking 30 cents for baskets of taro of similar quality ranging from twenty-five to forty pounds in weight and would probably manage to sell them all during the day. This would give a price for taro ranging from 0·75 cents to 1·2 cents per pound. Similarly small pineapples were usually priced at 10 cents while large ones cost 20 cents, but the range of weights of the pineapples which could be bought in either price category was great and in some cases overlapped. The rationale for valuing products such as pineapples and bunches of bananas by this first method is clearly centred on the fact that the size of the item cannot easily be adjusted. It is perhaps surprising that the range of weights of baskets of taro selling for the same price was so great, since it is quite simple for a vendor to alter the weight of the contents of a basket, but this was not generally done.

The second method which the vendor may use to value his produce is to group a number of items of the same product in such a way that they make up a lot which he estimates at prevailing market prices to be worth a convenient unit of money. In Kerema the unit was usually 10 cents. This method was frequently used to value produce such as oranges, eggs, crabs, and shellfish. For example, a vendor would group six small crabs into a lot worth 10 cents, while he would also make another lot of three large crabs and value them at 10 cents. This method probably leads to smaller variations in price than are encountered when produce is valued by the first method.

The price of betel nut did not vary greatly, principally because the size and quality of the nuts was comparatively uniform. It was generally traded at a price of 10 cents per dozen nuts and it was the only commodity which was traded in penny change.[5] For example, seven betel nuts were sold for 7d, but most of the betel nut transactions were nevertheless in units of 10 cents. The Administration paid a set price for each type of produce, but only prime quality food was bought. The price was usually higher than prevailing market prices.

There were indications that buyers selected their purchases in such a way that they paid a minimum price per unit of weight and in this way they consciously influenced the price which they paid. Unfortunately insufficient information was obtained to show clearly that this happened. There is little doubt that buyers selected for quality whenever possible. The produce which remained unsold at the end of a day was almost always inferior in some respect. Over-ripe bananas, green pineapples, and insect damaged taro were difficult to sell, while prime produce was quickly sold.[6]

I collected no firm evidence to show that prices were reduced towards the end of a market day and there did not appear to be any day-to-day reaction of prices to market conditions of supply and demand. One gets the impression that prices were inelastic largely because neither buyers nor sellers were heavily dependent on the market. If a vendor failed to sell his produce one could imagine him shrugging his shoulders, returning home and being none the worse for his day's outing. If a buyer failed to purchase a particular food he could in most cases go to his subsistence garden, harvest a similar item of food or a close substitute, and it would be unusual if he or his family were hungry on

[5]Trading at the time of the survey was entirely in Australian shillings and pence, hence a 'penny' here means an old penny, not a cent.

[6]The local people price traditional valuables according to quality; they are quick to detect even minor defects in shell ornaments and defective articles are accordingly priced lower than unblemished articles of similar size.

that particular day. In any case he could use the money which he intended to spend at the market, to buy food at one of the local retail stores.

A list of the estimated usual prices for commodities traded at the market appears in Table III. 8, but because the price for a particular commodity varied considerably within the market the information should be interpreted with caution. The table also shows for some commodities the corresponding prices at Koki market in Port Moresby.

Table III. 8 Market prices ruling at Kerema during the survey, with some comparison from Koki market, Port Moresby.* Prices are given in Australian shillings and pence (with decimal conversions), since goods were priced in this currency at the time of survey.

Produce	Kerema (s d)	Kerema (cents)	Koki (s d)	Koki (cents)
Sago (lb)	0 3	2.5	0 6	5.0
Colocasia taro (lb)	0 1	1.0	0 5	4.0
Sweet potatoes (lb)	0 2	1.7	0 7	5.9
Bananas (lb)	0 2	1.3	0 7	6.2
Breadfruit, large (each)	1 0	10.0	0 7	6.2
Breadfruit, small (each)	0 2 to 0 4	1.7 to 3.3		
Melons (each)	3 0 to 5 0	30.0 to 50.0		
Pineapples	1 0 to 2 0	10.0 to 20.0		
Oranges (each)	0 3 to 0 5	2.5 to 4.2		
Crabs (each)	0 6 to 1 0	5.0 to 10.0		
Eggs (each)	1 0	10.0		
Betel nuts (doz.)	1 0	10.0		
Peppers (bundle)	1 0	10.0		
Bread (loaf)	2 0	20.0		

*Koki market (Port Moresby) prices are from an unpublished survey by G. R. Spinks, except for sago, which is based on the author's informal investigations.

Conclusions

By 1963 the market had become an important part of the Kerema Bay cash economy and it was providing one of few opportunities available to inland people to engage in commercial activities locally. It was also a significant source of cash income for the people on the western shore of Kerema Bay. The people from the villages associated with the Cupisi project did not buy or sell large quantities of produce at the market. People employed at Kerema, together with Administration departments, provided the main buying force.

The market is characterised by an absence of competition between sellers and an absence of even rudimentary advertising. Similarly there is very little bargaining between buyers and sellers. Prices are variable within quite wide but rigid limits, and, while quality does not seem to influence price, it does influence a person's willingness to buy.

IV

Honiara Market and the Suppliers from Tasimboko West

I. Q. Lasaqa

This report is written from the point of view of the rural supplier of produce rather than around the market itself. In the course of research on the post-war development of the area of northern Guadalcanal known as Tasimboko West, it became apparent that a major source of income is provided by sale of goods in the town market at Honiara. The market was studied over a five-month period in 1966, but though data were collected on the whole operation of the market, emphasis was throughout on the suppliers from Tasimboko (Map 5).

Historical background

The area has had a violent recent history. Before World War II northern Guadalcanal had a few copra plantations, a scattered rural population, and nothing more. The only town in the British Solomon

This essay is part of a study focused on post-war Melanesian economic development in Tasimboko West, which is an electoral ward of the Guadalcanal Local Government Council. The field work was made possible by generous financial assistance from the Australian National University, for which grateful acknowledgment is made. I also wish to express my thanks to Dr H. C. Brookfield for his encouragement during its preparation and critical comments on an earlier draft. I must also record my appreciation of the assistance given by Mr J. O. L. Tedder, District Commissioner, Central Solomons, during the course of my field research. The co-operation and help of the local people were quite invaluable during the course of the market survey; to them I am deeply grateful. However, the views expressed in this essay must remain my responsibility.

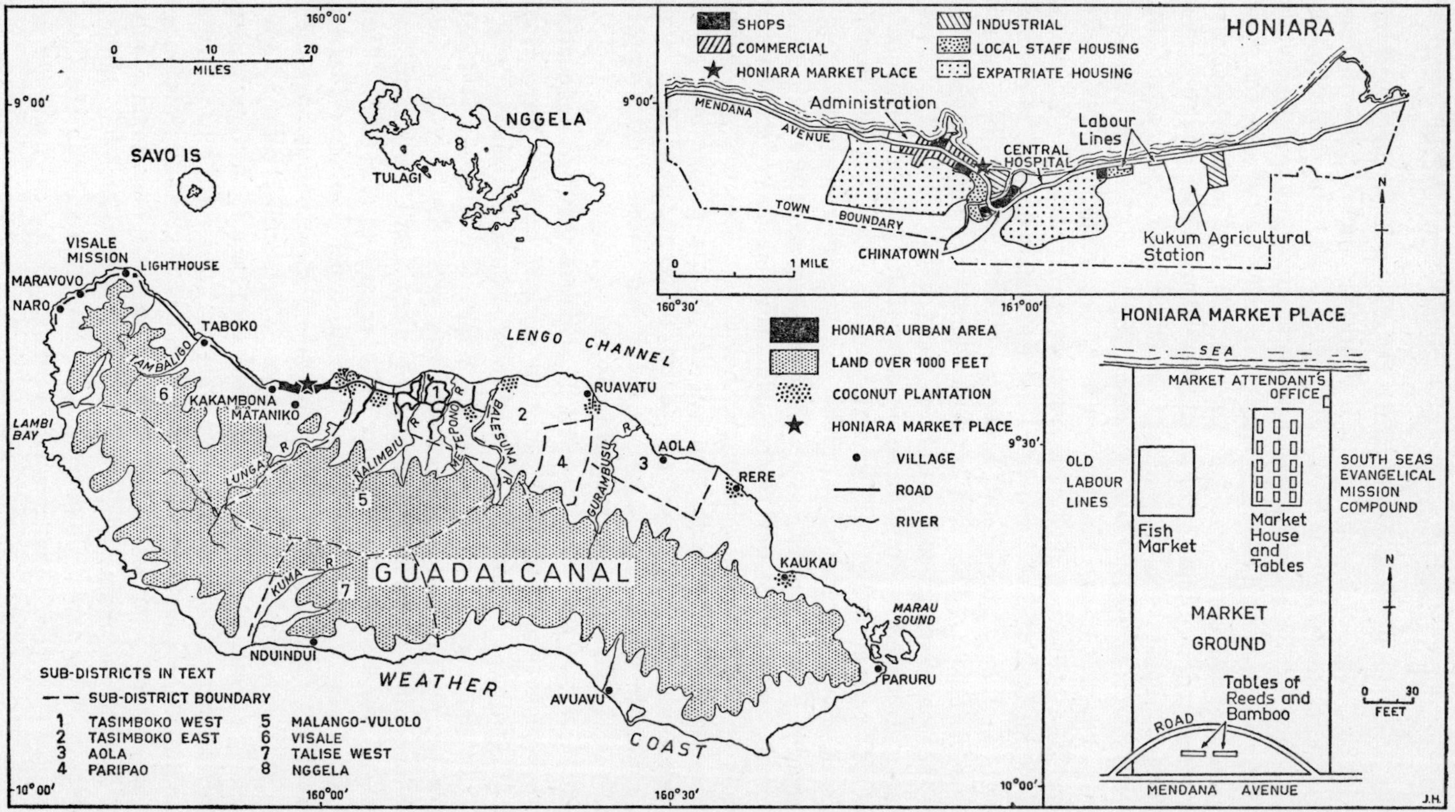

Map 5 *Guadalcanal Island, Solomons, showing Sub-districts, roads, and plantations (insets show Honiara town and Honiara market-place)*

Islands Protectorate was the capital, Tulagi, on a small island off Nggela, to the north of Guadalcanal. Northern Guadalcanal, the one large area of lowland plain in the Solomons, blossomed suddenly into prominence in 1942, when the Japanese occupiers began to build an airfield there to serve as a base for activities southward towards the New Hebrides and the Coral Sea. An American landing in mid-1942 was bitterly resisted, and until early 1943, Tasimboko West was the scene of one of the hardest-fought battles of the Pacific war. Several airfields were built, and later, after the Japanese withdrawal, a main American base was constructed at Point Cruz, a few miles west of the Tasimboko region. In 1945, when civil administration returned to the Solomons, much of this base was still standing, and the British authorities decided to establish the capital of the Protectorate here, rather than in the remains of Tulagi. The area between Point Cruz and the Balesuna River then possessed a good network of roads, with associated wharves, jetties, and airfields. Immovable military installations, particularly buildings, were in plenty. These were valuable assets to a government with little money immediately available for post-war reconstruction.

For a long time Honiara has relied for its very existence and expansion on the provision of government administration and other services; the bulk of its labour force, therefore, has always consisted of government employees. Only during the last decade did private enterprise, particularly in the building trade, enter the commercial field with an appreciable impact in the provision of much-needed extra opportunities for Melanesians to earn cash.

The Protectorate Labour Regulations stipulate that accommodation be provided by employers to Melanesian workers residing away from their villages, and permits the issue of rations, the cash value of which are to be deducted from the labourer's wages (WPHC 1963: 322). During the pre-war and immediate post-war years the issue of rations to Melanesian workers was universal practice. Until the second half of 1957, when a definite directive with regard to the use of local produce in labour rations was issued from the Chief Secretary, Western Pacific High Commission,[1] most government departments met their ration commitments by purchasing imported foodstuffs: polished Australian rice, white flour, and corned beef with cereal. Although post-war government ration scales have always provided for the use of local vegetables in lieu of rice, local staples and locally grown introduced vegetables were being used by a few government departments only. Clearly, what was permissible under the law was translated into administrative action by few Administration officers. Indeed, after the Chief Secretary had declared that it was government policy to encourage the

[1]Copies of a notice to this effect were sent to all Departmental Heads and District Commissioners.

purchase of local produce in lieu of rice, scepticism over the wisdom of the proposed change persisted among some government officers. The Commissioner, Central Solomons, for example, speaking about those for whose rations he was responsible, declared that the Melanesians would not welcome the proposed change.[2] And maybe he was right; but he did not explain the foundation of his opinion. However, he stressed the high degree of perishability of vegetable produce and the possibility of overstocking – admittedly not insuperable problems and amenable to administrative solution – as important factors to be considered in any change in ration issued. But he allows that the use of local produce would achieve some degree of economy. The Senior Medical Officer considered the imported diet to be inferior nutritionally, and it was by then involving government in a continued annual expenditure of $100,000 on rations from overseas.[3] The economic virtue of putting this money into local circulation is obvious enough; on the political plane, 'trade' in local foodstuffs with government would place the Administration in a more favourable light *vis-à-vis* the indigenes, and, in the long run, help to bridge the enormous gulf that separates the government from the governed.

The origin of Honiara market

Before 1957 the Medical, Prison, and Police Departments were already making local purchases of food for part of their ration issues. To see how this was done in the presence of unorganised indigenous producers requires a brief résumé of agricultural policy as it affected the production of local foodstuffs. As from 1 April 1949, a Commonwealth Development and Welfare grant was made available to establish on the former U.S. Army vegetable gardens at Ilu a demonstration and experimental farm. One of its aims was 'the early production of foodstuffs including rice, roots, ground nuts, vegetables, poultry and meat' (BSIP 1951– (1953: 3)). The residents of Honiara, and in particular government personnel, were the logical consumers of these products. In 1951, for instance, Ilu farm found little difficulty in disposing of its produce of root crops and vegetables. Of the 27 tons of sweet potatoes it harvested, 22 tons were sold to the Police, Prison, and Medical Departments and 5 tons used as stock feed; 280 pounds of the 300 pounds of vegetables produced were also sold (BSIP 1951– (1951: 8)). In 1949, too, approval was granted by the Colonial Office for the establishment at Kukum of an agricultural station. Clearing started early in 1950 and by the year's end it was producing large quantities of

[2]Central District Administration, correspondence on local food production.

[3]In fact the Senior Medical Officer took the initiative to point out the merits of using local produce as part of ration issues.

vegetables. Principally because large quantities of local produce were available from both Ilu and Kukum, and there was need of an organised channelling of produce disposal, the Department of Agriculture took the initiative and formally established a market-place. But it soon relinquished its control to the District Administration, which took interim charge until the Town Council was established in 1957. Thus organised marketing of local produce in Honiara owes its origin to Agriculture Department initiative in its attempt to dispose of its surplus produce after the needs of certain government institutions had been met. Although both Ilu and Kukum were established with the demonstration of improved agricultural methods under Solomon Islands conditions as a primary aim, the production patterns of these stations would suggest that the need to provide the fresh vegetable requirements of Honiara's population was the immediate objective and remained dominant, at least in the short term.

But by 1953 it had become increasingly and dishearteningly apparent that staff shortages and lack of machinery had made it difficult, if not impossible, for Ilu adequately to fulfil its functions as an experimental and demonstration farm. A decision was reached to discontinue the Ilu scheme and lease the property to private enterprise. This was effected in 1955. The discontinuance of the Ilu scheme, therefore, gave the first major opening to Melanesian producers to satisfy the demands of government institutions and other Honiara residents. And they were not found to be wanting. From Visale came European vegetables and some roots; a part-European family early supplied sweet potatoes to the Police barracks (BSIP 1957: 3). Longgu, Aola, and Tasimboko sent shiploads of root crops to both the Central Hospital and the Prison Department. In fact, so pressing was the need for vegetable produce after the closure of the Ilu scheme that the Medical Department made special efforts to obtain its supply of produce. During the first half of 1957, it let local producers know that it would purchase all and any produce brought at a price agreed upon by the District Commissioner.[4] This venture demonstrated that, given the opportunity and encouragement, local gardeners could and did produce more than enough for the requirements of that Department. By October 1957 the Senior Medical Officer indicated that the Central Hospital at Honiara was no longer able to guarantee the purchase of all produce offered to it. Supply had exceeded the demand in this one institution, due principally to the publicity it gave to its intention to purchase all available produce, and it was one of the few bulk consumers which did this at that time.

[4]In considering the use of local produce in labourers' diet, the experience of the Medical Department proved to be an effective factor. It showed that local producers were capable of meeting the demands of government institutions.

Early participants in Honiara market

Chiefly because of the high degree of perishability of local produce, long distances, and the scarcity of means of both land and sea transport until very recently, and the uncertainty of the weather, the opportunity to produce local foodstuffs for sale to Honiara's urban population was greatest for the favoured few who lived close to the town, or had reliable means of access to it either by launch and cutter or motor road transport. Naturally the areas least accessible to Honiara have tended to be excluded, although these regions, such as the 'weather coast' of Guadalcanal, were not completely ignored by the Administration. During the second half of 1958, and after some pressure from the Talise people through their representatives in the Guadalcanal Council, the District Administration made available its touring vessel once a month, with an administrative officer, to call at previously appointed points on Guadalcanal buying from the local people what produce they had to offer. But this experiment was short-lived. Economic considerations and the unpredictability of both quantity and kind of produce offered ruled it out. Weather restricted the operation of the vessel, especially on the south coast of Guadalcanal which is notorious for its high seas and strong winds at any time of the year, but particularly from March to September when these circum-insular market trips were undertaken.

These market trips were directed mainly at helping the 'weather coast' people. Other areas of Guadalcanal were left to find their own means of establishing a link with Honiara and government assistance to them did not go beyond the distribution of European vegetable seeds, which were never sufficient in the early years, and demonstrations of various machine implements at Kukum Agricultural Station. For Tasimboko the effect was that only the most enterprising individuals, and most especially those capable of securing reliable transport into Honiara, participated in the sale of local produce to Honiara's urban population, particularly the Melanesian sector. The N̄alimbiu River was not bridged until 1962 and the Metepono River in 1963.[5] Up to these dates only the western-most Tasimboko between Koli Point and Makile could sell local produce in Honiara with any degree of frequency. Arrangements were made with local Chinese traders whose trucks, launches, and cutters hauled the produce from the N̄alimbiu to Honiara. The most successful of the Tasimboko in this venture was Samuel Saki, the big man of Koli village. In his role as a contractor to South Pacific Traders in scrap metal collection between 1950 and 1953, he accumulated sufficient capital to purchase an ex-army jeep with a trailer. With the help of his supporters and kin he operated a vegetable

[5]Widespread flooding on the night of 15 November 1966 washed away the Metepono bridge.

farm at Oba, on the right bank of the N̄alimbiu, and supplied vegetables regularly to the Kwong Chow Hotel, occasionally to the Central Hospital at Honiara, to the Chinese community, and the town market itself. But Saki's case is atypical; it is a success story which was not quickly replicated. Important in this context, however, is the fact that the Tasimboko west of Balesuna did not at first need to sell produce in order to obtain cash. During 1950 to 1953 large numbers of people between Suagi and Makile were involved as contractors and labourers in the collection of brass shell cases, lead-covered cables, battery lead, copper radiators, gasoline and diesel oil drums, and marston mats for sale to the South Pacific Traders and K. H. Dalrymple Hay Pty Ltd. These Tasimboko, therefore, did not need other means to earn cash for the payment of the Council head tax ($1 in 1953)[6] and the purchase of Western goods which have for long acquired a necessity-status in their everyday life. Casual employment was available at Berande, Tetere, Tenaru, and Lunga copra estates, Ilu farm, and the Solomon Islands Timber Company at Tenakaro. The *mamata*[7] coconut groves provided a ready source of cash to many and those not in direct control of this resource could manipulate the appropriate social links and call on its accepted codes to share in the proceeds.

However, during the last decade, the links between Honiara and its eastern hinterland improved considerably. Roads have been extended and rivers bridged. Truck operators can now provide the services essential to a modern market economy and bring a greater number of people than before more frequently into Honiara market. More Tasimboko have taken advantage of this extra and hitherto more difficult opportunity to participate in the cash economy. This was welcome, for the scrap metal business came to an end, and labour opportunities stabilised at a lower level. The market grew for a variety of reasons. Following the abolition of the labour recruiting system after 1960, urban workers tended to stay longer on the job. Employers tended increasingly to pay wages in full cash value, and to discontinue the issue of rations (BSIP 1959: 3). Thus with reduced cash opportunities at home, and an expanding urban market made more accessible, more and more Tasimboko have availed themselves of Honiara market as a source of income.

The structure and organisation of Honiara market

Honiara's permanent market building was erected in 1959 at its present

[6]Minutes of the Guadalcanal Council Meeting, 18-21 November 1953.

[7]The *mamata* is the land-owning unit in Tasimboko and membership of it is traced through the female line. In the traditional situation customary law required that land and other immovable property were inherited through the *mamata* either individually or collectively.

site, by the main thoroughfare – Mendana Avenue – and staff were appointed for its maintenance and to collect a small fee of 20 cents per month from each seller. The building itself is open and small – some 60 feet by 30 feet with fifteen concrete slabs, each 6 feet by 3 feet and nearly 3 feet high, serving as tables. However, there is much open space into which producers and their wares can overflow (Map 5). In fact this is where the large majority of vendors conduct their business. They make do with the sand, or gravel-covered, or even bare ground, and grass lawn, for overnight accommodation. Allowing a minimum of ten square feet of space for each adult, the market house can ideally provide sleeping space for up to 140 people, but it is not unusual for this figure to be reduced to as low as 60, depending on the space taken up by the produce and other belongings of the early arrivals.

Honiara has no single market day; there is a distinct and overlapping pattern of bi-weekly and bi-monthly markets, the former patronised mainly by European buyers and sellers from peri-urban villages, the latter mainly by Melanesian buyers and by sellers from much further afield. The days and hours of doing business in the market are not laid down by law; it is permissible for a producer to bring his wares for sale to the market house at any time suitable to him. Hence the pattern has grown up by convenience rather than by regulation, and since Honiara Town Council has let it be known that it wants to see vendors bring produce to market more frequently, trade is spreading increasingly outside the established days.

The Tuesday and Saturday morning markets have persisted for a long time. It is customary for vendors to arrive in the early hours of the morning, sell the bulk of their produce before 8 a.m., and return home by midday. Only the villagers living within walking distance of the market, or with motor transport readily available, could hope to utilise these twice-weekly market occasions. Most favoured have been the people of Kakambona and Mataniko, west and south of Honiara respectively. Produce brought on those occasions is meant primarily to meet the demands of the town's European population and consequently consists chiefly of introduced vegetables. Agricultural extension work in the area just west of Honiara had the satisfaction of this demand as a principal aim for a time. Producers realise that their customers on these twice-weekly market mornings belong to a select group of town-dwellers who are the upper income group, and, most of them, expatriate Europeans.

The bulk of Honiara's Melanesian labour force receives a basic wage of \$16 to \$20 per month. As buyers of local produce they are more numerous during the middle- and end-of-month market periods, which conveniently coincide with government and private enterprise employees' pay-days. These are also periods during which large numbers of people from many areas bring produce to the market. Clearly, producers realise that their chances to earn money at these periods are much higher than during the twice-weekly market days. Many make a special effort to go to market on these occasions.

Unlike the normally brief affair of the twice-weekly market mornings, going to market at the middle and end of the month involves the seller in absences from his village of not less than two days, and up to six in some cases. The seller expects absences of this duration, and therefore equips himself, and his family if they accompany him, with bedding, cooking utensils, including firewood or a primus stove, and dry or cooked rations. Thus the market house and its environs become his temporary home. These two market periods are necessarily prolonged. They provide for a much expanded demand, in particular from the Melanesian sector of the population, while prospective buyers have large quantities and varieties of produce to choose from. Generally, producers believe that to arrive well before the labourers' pay-day is to have a better chance of quickly selling their produce; late arrivals face the uncertainties of a market-place situation in which total demand is as yet unknown. And sellers who intend to buy goods to take back to the village require a little time to wander through the main shops and inspect the assorted goods before they finally make their purchase. But perhaps the most important factor in the length of time a vendor spends in the market is a combination of the speed with which his produce is sold out and the availability of return transport. Also, a seller comes with a group and normally returns home with the same group and the group's departure time is mutually agreed upon by the truck or launch operator and his clients.

Data presented in this survey were collected during a period of five months. Altogether ten surveys were undertaken; the first at the end of March and the last during the middle of August 1966. After some observation it became apparent that the middle- and end-of-month market periods were the most important in terms of number of vendors, volume and variety of produce, and their origins. Hence the decision to confine the survey to these two periods. The survey was greatly assisted by the fact that there was no simultaneous arrival of producers in the market. Only five trucks, varying greatly in carrying capacity, were regularly involved in the carting of produce; they did not all start operations at once. Thus it was possible, with assistants recruited from the local people, to handle a truck-load of produce at a time and make a complete enumeration of every seller's produce before another truck-load arrived. Because nearly every seller on these occasions lived in the environs of the market for upwards of two days, it was possible to record the takings of each, together with unsold produce. What follows is a report on the findings of this survey of Honiara market, with particular attention to Tasimboko West's[8] position in the supply of produce, incomes of vendors, and the organisation and profitability of of marketing (Map 6).

Supply and suppliers of produce

All produce entering the Honiara market can be conveniently grouped into the following broad classes:

1. Root crops, which include the sweet potato, yam, *panna*, and taro.

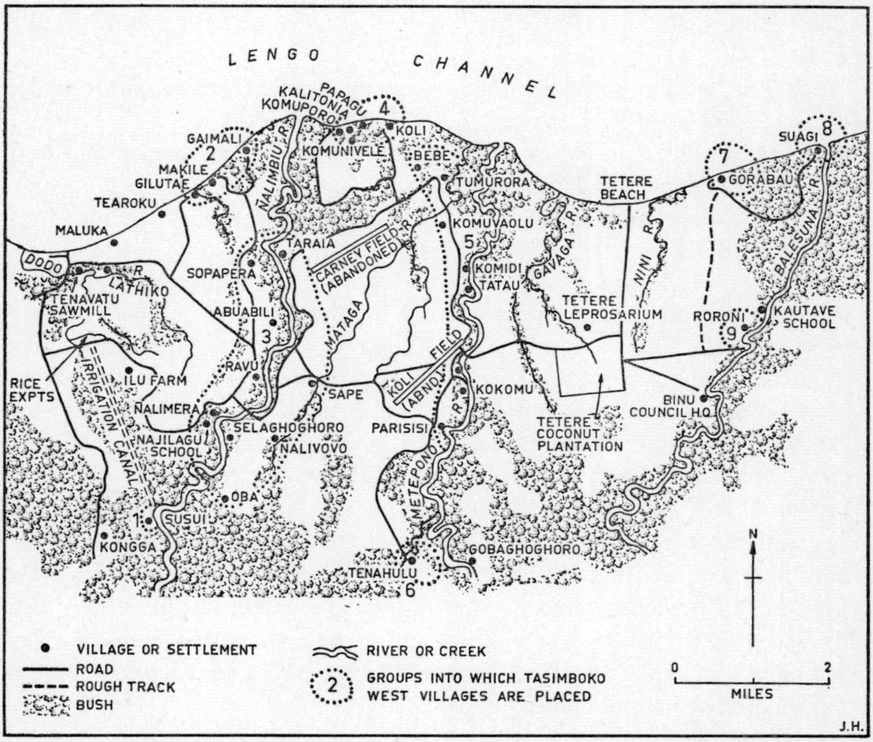

Map 6 *Tasimboko West, Guadalcanal, showing roads and villages supplying Honiara market*

[8]To help the discussion and comparison of data, Tasimboko West villages are placed under the following groups where generally similar villages and settlements are placed together: (1) Malaitan migrants – at Susui, Ravu, Abuabili, Taraia, Oba, Tearoku, and Lathiko; (2) Gilutae Gaimali – the two coastal villages by those names, including Makile; (3) N̄alimbiu – the Tasimboko of Sopapera, Abuabili, Ravu, N̄alimera, Najilagu, Selaghoghoro, N̄alivovo, and Taraia – on both sides of the N̄alimbiu River; (4) Koli Point – the villages of Komuporo, Kalitonia, Papagu, Komunivele, and Koli; (5) Metepono – the villages on the left bank of the Metepono River – Bebe, Tumurora, Komuvaolu, Tatau-Komidi, Kokomu, and Parisisi; (6) Tenahulu; (7) Gorabau; (8) Suagi; (9) Roroni.

2. Native vegetables, in particular *paura*[9] *(Hibiscus* spp.*)*, *kasume (Asplenium esculentum)*, *tavethi (Saccharum edule)*, and taro leaves.

3. Introduced vegetables such as Chinese cabbage, long and short beans, pumpkin and its leaves, tomatoes, pepper, lettuce, eggplant, cucumber, and watercress.

4. Fruits like watermelon, pineapple, pawpaw, oranges, lime, grapefruit, mangoes, and bananas; sugar cane, because of its use as a form of refreshment, is also included under this class.

5. Cooked foods — *ghola* (baked grated cassava), fish, pork, megapode and turtle eggs, and opossum.

6. Uncooked fish and meat, of which freshwater shells, giant coconut crabs, clam shells, pigs, ducks, and fowls were observed during this survey.

7. Nuts, including green and ripe coconuts, *sela* (*Canarium* almond), and *mega (Barringtonia edulis)*.

8. Traditional stimulants – *bua* (betel nut), *kura* (pepper leaf and vine), *poke* (lime), and twist tobacco.

9. Handiwork such as wooden bowls and baskets; pets (e.g. parrots) might also be included in this class.

Obviously this produce is offered to meet the dietary habits of specific, although not mutually exclusive, categories of buyers, namely the indigenous and non-indigenous, most of whom (and particularly the latter) do not produce any large part of their own requirements. Many Solomon Islanders employed in the town can produce some of their food requirements in Honiara; in 1964, for instance, 237 Melanesians were allotted garden sites on 296 acres specifically for that purpose (BSIP 1964: 7). It is not known how much food is produced in this way; it may be anything from one-fifth to one-quarter of the total consumed in any one month. There is a small though increasing minority of indigenous consumers who, as their incomes rise, are able to move towards a food consumption pattern which was once the monopoly of expatriate residents, and which is more varied than the traditional root-greens combination.

Roots

Whether measured in value or in volume, root crops comprised the bulk of all produce offered in the Honiara market during the periods surveyed (Table IV. 1). Altogether 6,468 baskets of roots, ranging between 60 pounds and 100 pounds per basket and valued at $1 to $2 per basket, were offered for sale, while a small proportion was brought specifically for relatives and friends in Honiara. Supply during the course of the survey indicates no marked monthly fluctuations; there

[9] Tasimboko vernacular is used throughout.

Table IV. 1 Percentage of the total produce by value in each produce class sold in Honiara market during the whole survey period

Produce class	% of total produce by value
Root crops	67·34
Native vegetables	1·06
European vegetables	1·84
Fruits	5·71
Cooked foods	8·12
Uncooked meat and fish	3·05
Nuts	4·77
Traditional stimulants	7·95
Handicrafts and pets	0·16
Total	100·00

was, however, a definite expansion in supply during the end-of-month market periods (Table IV. 2). In all, nearly 64 per cent of the total came during the end-of-month market periods while 36 per cent arrived during the mid-month period. This is a clear indication of the response by producers to the greater purchasing capacity of the Melanesian labour force pay packet at the end of the month, in comparison with the smaller number of workers (only those in non-government employment) who receive twice-monthly wages. Such an intra-month trough-crest pattern in the supply of root crops determines the pattern of total produce (Table IV. 3), and apparently correlates with the rise and fall in the total number of sellers at each market time (Table IV. 4). This rise-and-fall pattern applies also to each District represented in the survey with varying degrees of fluctuation that can often be explained. Thus the swelling of numbers from Tasimboko West at the end of June and July, and in mid-August, arose because large numbers of women from that area with little to sell, indeed sufficient only to meet

Table IV. 2 The supply of root crops to Honiara market at different market periods during the survey

Market period	Total baskets	Percentage
End of March	608	9·40
Mid-April	402	6·22
End of April	936	14·47
Mid-May	539	8·33
End of May	831	12·69
Mid-June	562	8·69
End of June	882	13·63
Mid-July	474	7·33
End of July	865	13·37
Mid-August	379	5·87
Total	6,468	100·00

Table IV. 3 Percentage of the total value of produce sold in Honiara market over the whole survey period, sold at each market period

Market period	Percentage
End of March	10·61
Mid-April	6·79
End of April	14·39
Mid-May	9·30
End of May	14·61
Mid-June	8·24
End of June	13·17
Mid-July	6·43
End of July	11·32
Mid-August	5·14
Total	100·00

their return fares and minor expenses, came to the market. These women came to visit their husbands and relatives who were on stevedore work in Honiara during June to August. The very low number from Visale at the mid-August survey was due in part to the timing of the survey after the mid-week market period was complete. Many from that area came to the mid-week market but had returned when the mid-August survey was taken.

Within this general frame, Tasimboko West's contribution is undoubtedly dominant in both number of sellers and volume of roots (Tables IV. 4 and IV. 5). On nearly all occasions it contributed upwards of 75 per cent of all root crops reaching the market. It is this dominance by Tasimboko West in the supply of roots which lies behind its superior position in terms of all produce together (Table IV. 6) for which its share is up to two-thirds. Significant factors in this dominant role are its productive alluvial soils, proximity to Honiara, and

Table IV. 4 Number of vendors in Honiara market by Districts at each market period during the survey

Market period	Tasimboko West	Tasimboko East	Visale	Malango	Paripao	Aola	Nggela	Talise West	Kukum	Total
End of March	66	13	39	4	13	7	—	—	—	141
Mid-April	41	1	41	1	—	—	—	—	—	84
End of April	83	19	37	—	8	12	1	—	—	160
Mid-May	43	1	28	4	—	11	—	5	—	92
End of May	87	38	43	5	7	—	1	—	1	182
Mid-June	58	4	37	—	—	—	—	—	—	99
End of June	92	42	57	7	12	—	4	—	—	215
Mid-July	40	9	21	5	—	—	—	—	—	75
End of July	100	19	25	3	5	—	—	—	—	152
Mid-August	58	—	17	3	3	—	—	—	—	81

Table IV. 5 Percentage of value of root crops sold in Honiara market for each market period, offered by vendors from each District, and from each group within Tasimboko West

Area	End Mar.	Mid-Apr.	End Apr.	Mid-May	End May	Mid-June	End June	Mid-July	End July	Mid-Aug.	Total
Malaitans	20·07	43·78	28·10	24·49	31·55	26·69	28·46	36·92	19·19	24·54	27·63
Gilutae-Gaimali	27·64	21·39	16·99	20·22	10·60	27·22	14·40	10·13	16·53	22·43	18·01
N̄alimbiu	12·50	7·46	16·45	8·90	7·80	17·44	5·90	18·99	20·35	24·27	13·61
Koli Point	9·54	6·22	7·16	7·98	3·90	5·16	2·49	—	7·05	2·64	5·36
Metepono	8·22	0·50	1·50	4·45	1·46	3·91	11·34	3·38	4·16	2·90	4·44
Tenahulu	0·49	—	—	—	14·01	—	—	—	—	—	1·82
Gorabau	2·48	2·24	0·10	5·94	2·92	1·07	1·25	3·38	1·51	4·75	2·24
Suagi	0·82	0·25	1·92	—	3·29	—	3·51	2·32	2·77	2·11	1·93
Roroni	0·16	—	3·31	2·23	4·87	6·41	7·48	4·85	16·07	10·29	5·98
Tasimboko West	81·92	81·84	75·53	74·21	80·40	87·90	74·83	79·97	87·63	93·93	81·02
Aola	8·22	—	8·33	16·14	—	—	—	—	—	—	3·32
Malango	0·99	—	0·21	2·23	2·31	—	4·08	2·10	6·36	4·49	2·43
Tasimboko East	0·82	—	5·24	—	7·67	2·85	9·41	0·63	3·93	—	3·92
Paripao	0·16	—	1·07	—	0·73	—	1·02	—	—	—	0·40
Visale	7·89	18·16	9·62	7·42	8·89	9·25	10·66	17·30	2·08	1·58	8·91
Total	100·00	100·00	100·00	100·00	100·00	100·00	100·00	100·00	100·00	100·00	100·00

Table IV. 6 Percentage of value of all produce sold in Honiara market for each market period, offered by vendors from each District, and from each group within Tasimboko West

Area	End Mar.	Mid-Apr.	End Apr.	Mid-May	End May	Mid-June	End June	Mid-July	End July	Mid-Aug.	% of total produce
Malaitans	13·49	28·30	20·11	15·79	19·58	22·38	22·13	30·50	16·62	21·03	20·26
Gilutae-Gaimali	21·84	7·10	14·99	14·82	7·67	23·77	11·78	9·58	13·93	21·42	14·95
N̄alimbiu	12·42	7·87	12·92	6·29	5·75	15·26	4·67	15·17	16·98	20·05	10·95
Koli Point	7·90	5·51	5·77	6·01	2·75	4·93	3·15	—	5·95	2·56	4·64
Metepono	5·87	1·13	2·08	3·44	4·86	3·10	10·88	3·76	4·83	4·52	4·74
Tenahulu	0·33	—	—	—	8·95	—	—	—	—	—	1·35
Gorabau	2·37	4·43	1·01	3·88	4·05	0·78	1·29	3·60	2·43	6·19	2·72
Suagi	0·61	1·83	1·88	—	2·22	—	2·86	1·99	4·33	2·09	1·88
Roroni	0·38	—	2·77	1·66	4·25	5·23	6·17	5·09	14·67	9·43	4·93
Tasimboko West	65·21	56·17	61·53	51·89	60·08	75·45	62·93	69·69	79·74	87·29	66·42
Aola	8·00	—	8·08	12·23	—	—	—	—	—	—	3·21
Malango	2·49	—	0·30	1·63	1·25	—	3·67	1·95	5·47	3·82	2·13
Tasimboko East	6·03	3·55	10·94	1·53	14·73	2·66	12·68	1·50	3·72	—	7·11
Paripao	2·74	—	1·75	—	1·70	—	3·44	—	4·74	—	1·82
Visale	15·53	40·28	16·13	14·28	17·72	21·89	16·27	26·86	6·33	8·89	16·71
Nggela	—	—	1·27	—	3·82	—	1·01	—	—	—	0·88
Talise West	—	—	—	18·44	—	—	—	—	—	—	1·71
Kukum	—	—	—	—	0·70	—	—	—	—	—	0·01
Total	100·00	100·00	100·00	100·00	100·00	100·00	100·00	100·00	100·00	100·00	100·00

the ease of arranging both sea and land transport. Immediately they are returned home certain producers make arrangements with particular truck operators whom they have come to patronise, to be collected for the next market day.

The contribution of Paripao District in both overall value and roots, but particularly the latter, clearly illustrates the predicament in which the interior inhabitants of Guadalcanal are placed in relation to the Honiara market. Many parts of Paripao are more than 40 miles from Honiara; and foot tracks wind over difficult terrain. What a producer from these distant parts offers for sale in the market-place must of necessity be limited to what he himself can carry to a point where road transport becomes available. His produce, which should not be too bulky or too heavy, must be of a kind that can command a high price, sufficient to compensate for the effort involved in its production, the burden of carrying it, and transport cost. Thus Paripao's contribution of roots consisted of taro sold at a rate of no less than 5 cents per pound, which is double the Administration's buying price for roots supplied to the Central Hospital and other places. For this reason, together with the relative prevalence of certain traditional skills, it is not surprising that nearly all the articles of indigenous manufacture (baskets and wooden bowls) and parrots were contributed by Paripao villagers.

However, the most interesting fact in Tasimboko West's dominance is that it is not wholly contributed by the Tasimboko themselves. This has a tinge of irony in it; no less than one-fifth to one-quarter of all roots supplied during any one market time and for all dates together, and one-fifth of all produce (Tables IV. 5 and IV. 6), came from Malaitan migrants resident in Tasimboko West. These Malaitans are dependent on either government or the Tasimboko, but initially entirely on the Tasimboko, for their right to use land. The migrants have come to settle in the District only since about 1963 and, unlike the Tasimboko, the sale of garden produce in Honiara is the main, and for many, the only way of earning money open to them. Thus, it is not surprising that in terms of frequency of attendance (Table IV. 7), theirs is the highest percentage of producers selling at the market-place

Table IV. 7 **Frequency of attendance at Honiara market during the survey** period by vendors from each main District and by Malatan vendors from Tasimboko West

Attendance frequency range	Visale (%)	Tasimboko West (%)	Malaitans (%)	Tasimboko East (%)	Malango (%)	Paripao (%)	Aola (%)
1–3	96·67	77·63	53·33	99·07	90·63	100	100
4–6	2·50	17·98	20·00	—	9·37	—	—
7–10	0·83	4·39	26·67	0·93	—	—	—

during seven or more of the periods surveyed. Distance and transport problems are major factors in the infrequent attendances of Paripao and Aola producers. The percentages for Visale and Tasimboko West reflect a situation in which other cash-earning alternatives are available so that despite the presence of transport links there is, on the whole, no urgent necessity to produce foodstuffs for sale in the Honiara market.

Cooked foods

In the supply of cooked foods Tasimboko West's dominant role shows tremendous monthly and intra-monthly fluctuations; in the result its total contribution, a little over one-third, is only slightly higher than that of Visale (Table IV. 8). Tasimboko West's share of cooked foods comprised mainly *ghola*, in which all areas are represented, although the bulk came from the villages west of Koli Point. Megapode (*Megapodius freycinet eremita Hartlaub* spp.) and turtle eggs, the bulk of which came during May and June, are the speciality of Gorabau and Suagi, particularly the former, whose megapode field between the village and Tetere landing is a closely guarded asset and a valuable source of protein. Tasimboko East is also known for megapode eggs, although the area offered no competition with Gorabau in the market. Cooked foods from Visale are the most varied of any district. *Ghola* apart, baked fish and pork were the next most frequently offered, especially during the end-of-month market occasions. Visale supplied the bulk of all the baked fish which reached the Honiara market except at the end of May. These fish abound in its numerous small sheltered bays and fringing reefs – a coastline morphological feature conspicuously absent east of Honiara. Sellers from Nggela also contributed a fair proportion of the total baked fish sold, particularly at the end of May when baked fish from the Sandfly area comprised over 60 per cent of the total offered. And although these arrived two days after pay-day, it took less than three hours to dispose of this produce. Its popularity among Melanesians is obvious.

Cooked foods sold in the Honiara market are obviously directed at the purse and eating habits of the indigenous consumer, and especially the single or unaccompanied worker, who shares a room in one of the dormitory-like government and private labour lines at Kukum. On the afternoon of pay-day, he finishes work some time between 4.00 and 4.30 p.m.; rather than cook his own evening meal, he goes 'walk about 'long' market-place. If early, he will certainly buy some baked pork, or fish, or megapode eggs, depending on variety and amount still unsold. If these are sold out, he might have to eat *ghola* without the traditional and more nutritious foods, or resort to tinned meat or fish as a second ingredient in his evening meal. On many occasions cooked

Table IV. 8 Percentage of value of cooked foods sold in Honiara market for each market period, offered by vendors from each District, and from each group within Tasimboko West

Area	End Mar.	Mid-Apr.	End Apr.	Mid-May	End May	Mid-June	End June	Mid-July	End July	Mid-Aug.	Total
Malaitans	—	—	1·35	—	—	—	2·92	—	—	4·26	0·85
Gilutae-Gaimali	15·31	0·58	8·99	10·15	1·94	49·02	8·31	—	—	27·13	8·45
N̄alimbiu	15·38	14·83	5·17	—	1·46	19·61	3·07	—	—	7·75	5·97
Koli Point	7·29	6·46	1·35	—	0·73	5·88	2·31	—	—	—	2·56
Metepono	0·80	1·90	3·34	—	—	—	21·62	—	5·98	—	4·79
Tenahulu	—	—	—	—	—	—	—	—	—	—	—
Gorabau	3·61	4·37	8·83	5·23	11·01	—	1·31	7·55	12·35	10·47	6·90
Suagi	—	—	2·39	—	1·02	—	3·07	—	4·78	3·88	1·63
Roroni	2·16	—	0·16	3·08	4·90	—	—	—	14·74	19·38	3·39
Tasimboko West	44·55	28·14	31·58	18·46	21·06	74·51	42·61	7·55	37·85	72·87	34·54
Aola	0·80	—	4·38	—	—	—	—	—	—	—	0·83
Malango	8·01	—	0·40	—	1·02	—	3·24	16·04	2·39	—	2·53
Tasimboko East	10·82	—	11·14	—	26·30	4·90	29·15	17·92	29·28	—	17·64
Paripao	4·33	—	—	—	2·13	—	0·62	—	—	—	1·36
Visale	31·49	71·86	38·98	81·54	19·65	20·59	20·54	58·49	30·48	27·13	32·38
Nggela	—	—	13·52	—	25·23	—	3·84	—	—	—	9·50
Kukum	—	—	—	—	4·61	—	—	—	—	—	1·22
Total	100·00	100·00	100·00	100·00	100·00	100·00	100·00	100·00	100·00	100·00	100·00

foods purchased in the market-place are consumed there; but even if he prefers to eat his meal in his quarters, the labourer normally does not leave for home soon after he has made his purchase. Most likely he has to walk back, and he is in no great hurry to do this. The market-place is where he expects to meet some of his own people and acquaint himself with the latest news from home. Indeed, someone from his own village may have a message for him from a close relative; others will renew old acquaintances and make the habitual offering to share in the traditional stimulants – betel, pepper leaf or vine, and lime. In return he might offer a roll of his Rothman King Size Filter cigarette. And when he finally returns to the labour line he is certain to take with him some of these traditional stimulants – either bought or given by friends and relatives.

Traditional stimulants

Of all produce reaching Honiara market, the traditional stimulants form a group apart that are exclusively for ultimate indigenous consumption. Chinese traders rank high as bulk buyers of this produce class, especially the betel which has a high keeping quality. It is then retailed to the town Melanesian at eight to ten nuts for 10 cents, depending on size.

Of all the produce classes here identified to which Tasimboko West makes some contribution, this is the group in which its share of the total is the lowest – only 10 per cent (Table IV. 9). Not a single village group in Tasimboko West contributed 2 per cent or more of the total supplied during the whole survey. In Tasimboko West there is a shortage of betel for local consumption, let alone for sale. It is not uncommon for the Tasimboko whose origins are traceable to the interior villages to send word to their kin, if they do not go there themselves, for some betel to be brought. The war completely transformed the Tasimboko landscape and left it devoid of native village settlements. The westward migration of the population after the war was slow. With village sites destroyed many new locations were chosen and fresh plantings of betel made. The tree takes six to eight years to fruit and ceases to be productive after twenty years. The betel palm, therefore, has a total effective life of a little over ten years. There is a scarcity of bearing betel palm in Tasimboko West. To acquire betel nut two choices are open to the people: they must either walk through bush tracks over difficult terrain to Tasimboko bush and pick the betel from the groves of their relatives there, or obtain it locally through the manipulation of the appropriate social links and customary procedures. Both courses of action are followed. Although these choices apply to

Tasimboko West as a whole they vary in degree of force in different areas, depending on the available supply and local circumstances. Thus Tasimboko West's traditional stimulant contribution was largely pepper leaves and vine, gathered wild from nearby secondary bush, and nowhere is this more apparent, and for obvious reasons, than in the case of the recently settled Malaitan migrants of Susui, Ravu, and Taraia.

Visale and Tasimboko East supplied the bulk of traditional stimulants; between them they account for more than 50 per cent of the total. Talise West's single but prominent contribution was in the form of large quantities of local twist tobacco of which a very small proportion was actually disposed of in the Honiara market. The bulk was returned home after some attempt at hawking it at Savo Island and the littoral villages west from Visale Mission. Paripao's share of the total is significantly higher than that of Tasimboko West, and most particularly at the end of July, when it contributed two-thirds of the total supplied, with betel dominating on that occasion. Because of its wide area of reef, Visale bulked large in the supply of lime.

Fruits

Tasimboko West reasserts its prominent position in the provision of fruits; it contributed more than 63 per cent of the total (Table IV. 10). Much of this consisted of watermelon from the Metepono area, particularly from Kokomu village, which supplied 50 per cent of the fruits available at the end of May (nearly all watermelon), from Roroni, and and from the Malaitans at Ravu and Susui. The Gilutae-Gaimali group provided the bulk of the pineapple reaching the market on most occasions, while large quantities of sugar cane came from the N̄alimbiu area, especially Selaghoghoro settlement. Bananas came from virtually all areas within and without Tasimboko West but Visale predominated in the supply of ripe bananas. Visale producers are notable for the variety of fruits they offer for sale at any one time, and, unlike Tasimboko West, vendors do not specialise in the sale of any one type of fruit.

Coconuts and other nuts

The supply of coconuts to the Honiara market came largely from Tasimboko West and Visale, with the former having the edge over the latter; between them they contributed 88 per cent of the total (Table IV. 11). This is a direct reflection of the abundance of this resource in these two areas. Its sale is not confined to those in direct control of palms; men 'ask and give' coconuts for sale in the market. This transfer of produce from owner to non-owner for the latter's

Table IV. 9 Percentage of value of traditional stimulants sold in Honiara market for each market period, offered by vendors from each District, and from each group within Tasimboko West

Area	End Mar.	Mid-Apr.	End Apr.	Mid-May	End May	Mid-June	End June	Mid-July	End July	Mid-Aug.	Total
Malaitans	5·17	—	2·14	—	—	1·69	1·86	—	2·66	8·77	1·48
Gilutae-Gaimali	3·44	—	9·21	—	—	—	1·44	—	1·33	8·77	1·47
N̄alimbiu	4·55	—	—	—	—	13·11	—	—	4·38	2·19	1·69
Koli Point	2·03	—	—	0·50	—	—	3·22	—	1·99	2·63	1·07
Metepono	—	—	3·64	—	—	—	—	—	—	—	0·22
Tenahulu	0·47	—	—	—	5·63	—	—	—	—	—	0·72
Gorabau	—	—	—	—	—	—	2·54	—	—	10·97	0·97
Suagi	—	—	1·50	—	—	—	—	—	7·30	—	0·81
Roroni	—	—	—	—	1·21	—	0·25	6·44	4·65	—	1·09
Tasimboko West	15·66	—	16·49	0·50	6·84	14·80	9·31	6·44	22·31	33·33	9·52
Aola	23·47	—	42·82	7·34	—	—	—	—	—	—	6·51
Malango	—	—	—	1·00	0·16	—	—	—	2·19	—	0·51
Tasimboko East	44·29	23·46	6·64	—	53·86	6·34	45·81	17·17	—	—	22·00
Paripao	7·82	—	—	—	9·56	—	19·48	—	66·50	—	11·80
Visale	8·76	76·54	34·05	10·84	29·58	78·86	25·40	76·39	9·00	66·67	28·67
Talise West	—	—	—	80·32	—	—	—	—	—	—	20·99
Total	100·00	100·00	100·00	100·00	100·00	100·00	100·00	100·00	100·00	100·00	100·00

financial benefit takes place within a framework of reciprocal obligations, although the object is market trade. The dominant role of Visale and Tasimboko West in the supply of coconuts reflects their ease of access to Honiara, in marked contrast to Tasimboko East, also possessing vast stretches of coconut groves but handicapped by relatively difficult and less frequent means of transport to the town. For Tasimboko East the number of coconuts offered for sale in Honiara largely depends on what can be carried by the vendor or transported by canoe, along with other produce, to the landing at Suagi or Tetere beach. From here the remainder of the journey to Honiara is by truck. The alternative to selling coconuts is making copra for sale to the local Chinese trader – Lo See War – who buys copra in this area every week and pays cash on the spot.

The relative advantages of selling coconuts whole in the market or of making copra in the village for sale to visiting buyers thus vary with distance from the market, and with the time-budget of the individual. Making copra is time-consuming work, and returns are lower than those obtained from selling green or ripe nuts. Further, cash is more quickly obtained from selling the nuts without processing. On the other hand, the carriage of nuts to market is arduous if porterage is involved over any part of the journey, and fewer nuts can be handled than in copra-making.

During this survey very little *Canarium* almond arrived for sale, due chiefly to the fact that it was out of season. Some *Barringtonia edulis*, however, came from Visale, both Tasimboko West and East, and Paripao. These sold at the same rate as betel nut, 10 cents for twelve.

Uncooked fish and meat

Among produce consistently sold in the Honiara market during the survey, the uncooked foods, as categorised here, displayed a unique variability; not a single item in this class reached the market-place during the mid-June and mid-August surveys (Table IV. 12). The presence or absence of items of uncooked foods for sale indicates, perhaps more clearly than for any other category of produce, the sorts of calculation, economic and otherwise, the producer is involved in when contemplating a market outing. Obviously, uncooked foods of the variety offered are important sources of protein in the village diet and, more importantly, and unlike the coconut, they are not easy to come by; the pig in particular had a high value in traditional society, now transferred to monetary terms with much inflation in the process. The sale of uncooked foods, therefore, is the expression of a choice by the producer after due consideration of two sets of factors: the urgency of his need for cash and for things only cash can obtain on the one

Table IV. 10 Percentage of value of fruits sold in Honiara market for each market period, offered by vendors from each District, and from each group within Tasimboko West

Area	End Mar.	Mid-Apr.	End Apr.	Mid-May	End May	Mid-June	End June	Mid-July	End July	Mid-Aug.	Total
Malaitans	8·37	5·09	4·88	7·30	6·88	36·04	18·34	35·67	45·45	31·68	13·96
Gilutae-Gaimali	18·20	13·77	14·62	11·92	5·09	2·35	3·45	0·58	—	9·94	9·20
N̄alimbiu	19·78	12·43	14·62	7·83	7·73	14·05	—	—	—	—	9·79
Koli Point	4·98	4·64	13·61	14·24	1·89	1·98	10·90	—	—	4·35	6·38
Metepono	6·92	3·14	4·37	5·33	50·90	3·24	0·14	—	16·97	30·43	14·03
Tenahulu	—	—	—	—	—	—	—	—	—	—	—
Gorabau	2·67	6·74	—	—	1·41	—	—	—	0·61	—	1·51
Suagi	—	9·88	0·34	14·24	—	—	0·28	5·26	—	—	2·90
Roroni	0·12	—	8·59	—	4·71	10·99	14·90	18·72	4·85	1·24	5·71
Tasimboko West	61·04	55·69	61·03	60·86	78·61	68·65	48·01	60·23	67·88	77·64	63·48
Aola	0·24	—	—	—	—	—	—	—	—	—	0·04
Malango	8·37	—	0·17	4·98	—	—	6·76	—	—	—	2·68
Tasimboko East	7·04	21·41	21·85	21·35	12·35	—	31·17	—	7·27	—	14·94
Paripao	5·46	—	6·05	—	0·09	—	3·31	—	—	—	1·93
Visale	17·85	22·90	10·90	12·81	8·95	31·35	10·75	39·77	24·85	22·36	16·93
Total	100·00	100·00	100·00	100·00	100·00	100·00	100·00	100·00	100·00	100·00	100·00

hand, and his subsistence and ceremonial demands on the other. Provided other factors, such as transport and the external demand, remain reasonably stable, the sale of uncooked foods of the kinds encountered, for which there is an insatiable demand by Honiara's Melanesian population, implies either abundance of the food or a pressing immediate need for cash, or both, operating in different degrees at different times for different sellers and also for a single seller. Important, too, is the time of the month in which a particular market trip falls; and on these particular mid-month occasions when no uncooked foods were offered, efforts to produce something for sale are usually at a minimum.

Another unusual feature of this group of items is that for the first time Tasimboko East's contribution exceeded those of all other groups taken individually though not collectively. The bulk of the Tasimboko East contribution, like that of almost all other source areas, was by way of fowl, a valuable food item sold at $1 per bird. In contrast to roots, low bulk and high value adequately compensate for the distance covered and freight rate (15 cents per bird) and still leave a sufficiently remunerative reward. Tasimboko East's only other contribution to uncooked foods was the shellfish of its inter-tidal mangrove flats, particularly those about the mouths of the Berande and Taivu Rivers. In Tasimboko West, only the Metepono villages are favoured with an abundance of shellfish, gathered from Mataga Creek. Nggela's small single contribution consisted of giant coconut crabs sold at the end of May. This item of food is considered a delicacy among islanders and therefore appropriately commanded a high price – $1 to $1.50 each for the largest.

Native and European vegetables

Last but not least of the major groups of produce are the vegetables, both native and introduced. Within Tasimboko West, the most striking feature of vegetable supply is that nearly all Tasimboko West vegetables come from villages west of Koli Point, Malaitan contribution included (Tables IV. 13 and IV. 14). Although Tasimboko West's total contributions at certain dates were as high as 40 per cent or more, its total contribution for the whole period of the survey is small, especially in the supply of introduced vegetables. In the absence of means of artificial preservation and given the uniformly high day temperatures of the Solomon Islands, vegetables suffer very high rates of deterioration; with long distances and poor transport between the town consumer and the rural supplier, the risk of wastage during the period between picking and arrival in the market-place is obviously high. Thus the supply of vegetables tends to be related to the distance from and the availability of an efficient link with the town. To take an extreme case,

Table IV. 11 Percentage of value of coconuts sold in Honiara market for each market period, offered by vendors from each District, and from each group within Tasimboko West

Area	End Mar.	Mid-Apr.	End Apr.	Mid-May	End May	Mid-June	End June	Mid-July	End July	Mid-Aug.	Total
Malaitans	—	—	—	—	—	—	5·18	—	—	—	0·58
Gilutae-Gaimali	16·52	26·86	29·03	36·09	11·93	33·35	3·52	19·66	4·92	25·48	19·17
N̄alimbiu	—	—	—	—	—	1·97	1·28	—	—	—	0·38
Koli Point	6·24	6·73	1·14	—	3·58	11·69	1·73	—	0·63	3·23	3·57
Metepono	3·27	—	5·53	13·06	—	—	8·90	15·21	13·95	18·60	7·21
Tenahulu	—	—	—	—	—	—	—	—	—	—	—
Gorabau	4·21	14·29	2·28	—	10·08	—	—	10·30	10·15	21·07	6·82
Suagi	2·34	8·09	5·32	—	1·79	—	—	—	19·98	3·23	4·74
Roroni	—	—	—	3·73	2·51	2·41	2·50	7·02	4·70	3·23	2·55
Tasimboko West	32·58	55·97	43·30	52·88	29·89	49·42	23·11	52·19	54·33	74·84	45·02
Aola	—	—	7·43	2·33	—	—	—	—	—	—	1·10
Malango	—	—	—	—	—	—	—	—	—	—	—
Tasimboko East	2·57	—	7·76	—	15·04	0·86	36·88	9·59	17·12	—	10·59
Paripao	1·40	—	—	—	—	—	5·57	—	—	—	0·76
Visale	63·45	44·03	41·51	44·79	55·07	49·72	34·44	38·22	28·55	25·16	42·53
Total	100·00	100·00	100·00	100·00	100·00	100·00	100·00	100·00	100·00	100·00	100·00

many Aola producers must spend at least a whole day preparing produce for sale, then negotiate up to three miles of the braided course of the Gurambusu River to get to a point where a launch or cutter boat, invariably previously arranged, can collect and ship their produce to Honiara. Even then the weather may not be at all to their advantage. Aola, not surprisingly, contributed no vegetables at all to the Honiara market. On the other hand, road and rapid motor transport make possible the sale of vegetables from points of origin twenty-five to thirty miles west of the capital, if they are on or near the main road. But this alone does not adequately explain Visale's prominent role as a supplier of vegetables, particularly introduced vegetables, and the poverty of the supply from other parts of the region. One must examine official agricultural extension policy and actual practice during the last decade.

The Agricultural Department has always been bedevilled by staff shortages, especially at the field officer level and above; therefore it has had to make the best possible use of its small and often over-taxed staff.[10] During the last fifteen years at least, numerous technical and administrative officers of government toured east Guadalcanal as far as Marau Sound; the more daring have crossed the island and followed the southeast coast from Avuavu to Paruru, where they were picked up by a government vessel. Tremendous distances were covered under very trying physical conditions; but it was impossible to know this vast and complex area in depth. Besides, these tours had specific objectives. Reports on the tours rightly single out for example and praise the struggle of the interior villager to produce cash crops, but, through inadequate appreciation of all the problems involved and failure to see the situation as the inhabitants themselves saw it, condemn the 'economic apathy' and 'indolence' of the coastal people, particularly the Tasimboko, both East and West. Little did most touring officers realise that during and after the war these people enjoyed a very high level of cash earning which, in relation to pre-war standards and those prevailing in other less fortunate rural areas, can be regarded as sufficient for 'primitive' affluence. Cash-crop cultivation involved a wait plus maintenance period upwards of six years, so other and more lucrative short-term means of obtaining money were pursued. The long-term prospects of cash-crop cultivation did not enter into the people's calculation of objectives and means of achieving them. Unfortunately, behaviour resulting from

[10]Early in 1959, for example, the official duties of the Agricultural Officer, Central Solomons, apart from responsibility for all agricultural work in his district, included the following: responsibility for agricultural work in the Eastern District, Kukum Agricultural Station and staff training there, the compilation of departmental radio programs, livestock work in the Solomons generally, maintaining contact with Protectorate extension work generally, and assisting the Chief Agricultural Officer in other specific tasks. The wide-ranging nature of these duties and their complexity speak for themselves.

Table IV. 12 Percentage of value of uncooked foods sold in Honiara market for each market period, offered by vendors from each District, and from each group within Tasimboko West

Area	End Mar.	Mid-Apr.	End Apr.	Mid-May	End May	Mid-June	End June	Mid-July	End July	Mid-Aug.	Total
Malaitans	—	—	—	6·67	1·39	—	—	—	—	—	0·68
Gilutae-Gaimali	—	—	—	—	—	—	—	—	—	—	—
N̄alimbiu	6·90	—	—	—	—	—	—	—	—	—	0·68
Koli Point	6·90	—	—	—	—	—	6·35	—	—	—	2·05
Metepono	—	16·67	3·13	—	4·17	—	14·29	—	12·12	—	6·83
Tenahulu	—	—	—	—	—	—	—	—	—	—	—
Gorabau	—	58·33	—	—	19·44	—	1·56	80·00	—	—	8·87
Suagi	—	8·33	—	—	—	—	—	—	36·37	—	4·44
Roroni	—	—	—	—	6·95	—	—	—	12·12	—	3·07
Tasimboko West	13·80	83·33	3·13	6·67	31·95	—	22·20	80·00	60·61	—	26·62
Aola	44·83	—	—	80·00	—	—	—	—	—	—	8·53
Malango	—	—	—	—	—	—	50·80	—	—	—	10·92
Tasimboko East	20·69	—	79·69	13·33	50·00	—	23·82	—	33·33	—	41·30
Paripao	6·90	—	12·50	—	9·72	—	—	—	—	—	5·80
Visale	13·78	16·67	4·68	—	7·24	—	3·18	20·00	6·06	—	6·82
Nggela	—	—	—	—	1·09	—	—	—	—	—	0·01
Total	100·00	100·00	100·00	100·00	100·00	—	100·00	100·00	100·00	—	100·00

Table IV. 13 Percentage of value of native vegetables sold in Honiara market for each market period, offered by vendors from each District, and from each group within Tasimboko West

Area	End Mar.	Mid-Apr.	End Apr.	Mid-May	End May	Mid-June	End June	Mid-July	End July	Mid-Aug.	Total
Malaitans	6·64	—	10·68	6·60	2·92	13·79	13·02	—	—	20·00	6·84
Gilutae-Gaimali	22·45	21·58	—	16·98	3·65	—	5·48	16·36	—	11·43	11·69
N̄alimbiu	24·49	2·16	—	15·09	0·73	—	—	16·36	—	11·43	8·03
Koli Point	3·57	2·16	—	1·89	—	—	4·79	—	—	—	1·88
Metepono	—	—	—	—	—	—	—	—	—	—	—
Tenahulu	—	—	—	—	—	—	—	—	—	—	—
Gorabau	—	—	—	—	—	—	—	—	—	—	—
Suagi	—	—	—	—	—	—	—	—	—	—	—
Roroni	—	—	—	—	—	—	—	—	26·47	—	0·89
Tasimboko West	57·15	25·90	10·68	40·56	7·30	13·79	23·29	32·72	26·47	42·86	29·33
Aola	—	—	—	—	—	—	—	—	—	—	—
Malango	9·18	—	—	—	10·22	—	8·22	—	—	22·86	5·15
Tasimboko East	—	—	—	—	9·49	—	4·79	—	—	—	1·98
Paripao	—	—	—	—	—	—	—	—	—	—	—
Visale	33·67	74·10	89·32	59·44	72·99	86·21	63·70	67·28	73·53	34·28	63·54
Total	100·00	100·00	100·00	100·00	100·00	100·00	100·00	100·00	100·00	100·00	100·00

Table IV. 14 Percentage of value of European vegetables sold in Honiara market for each market period, offered by vendors from each District, and from each group within Tasimboko West

Area	End Mar.	Mid-Apr.	End Apr.	Mid-May	End May	Mid-June	End June	Mid-July	End July	Mid-Aug.	Total
Malaitans	—	—	0·85	—	0·23	—	0·52	6·42	44·74	—	1·59
Gilutae-Gaimali	3·74	—	0·43	7·09	—	—	—	—	—	10·81	1·08
N̄alimbiu	15·89	12·68	17·95	4·26	7·42	—	3·14	—	—	32·43	8·44
Koli Point	2·80	2·17	0·43	—	—	0·93	—	—	—	—	0·68
Metepono	—	—	—	—	—	—	—	—	—	—	—
Tenahulu	—	—	—	—	—	—	—	—	—	—	—
Gorabau	—	—	—	—	—	—	—	—	—	—	—
Suagi	—	—	—	—	—	—	—	—	—	—	—
Roroni	—	—	0·43	—	—	—	2·09	—	—	—	0·28
Tasimboko West	22·43	14·85	20·09	11·35	7·65	0·93	5·75	6·42	44·74	43·24	12·07
Aola	—	—	—	—	—	—	—	—	—	—	—
Malango	—	—	6·41	—	0·96	—	—	—	—	13·51	1·36
Tasimboko East	—	—	—	—	1·20	—	26·70	—	2·63	—	2·23
Paripao	—	—	—	—	—	—	0·52	—	—	—	0·05
Visale	77·57	85·15	73·50	88·65	90·19	99·07	67·03	93·58	52·63	43·25	84·29
Total	100·00	100·00	100·00	100·00	100·00	100·00	100·00	100·00	100·00	100·00	100·00

such short-term objectives, although sound within its limits, was wrongly analysed and labelled by government extension workers. Government policy regarding land in the area and the people's reaction to it aggravated the situation further, and made the position of the agricultural extension worker, a government agent in the eyes of the Tasimboko, completely untenable. For these reasons, continued agricultural extension work among Melanesians has not, until very recently, been a feature of the area east of Honiara. West of Honiara, however, government officers, and in particular officers of the Department of Agriculture, have found the people 'co-operative' and 'responsive' to advice. So this is one of the areas in which agricultural extension work was first commenced, with operations based from Honiara. From the point of view of vegetable supply, and especially after Ilu ceased to operate under government control and when Kukum became more diversified in function with low priority for vegetable production, Visale became the obvious target for a 'produce-more-vegetables' extension program campaign. As a result, Visale contributes upwards of 80 per cent, sometimes 90 per cent and more, of all the vegetables offered to meet the taste of the Europeans and the best paid and more sophisticated Melanesians resident in Honiara.

Unsold produce

In a market-place like that of Honiara, where regular attendance of producers in large numbers is a very recent practice,[11] where a not inconsiderable number of town Melanesians produce some of their own food requirements, and where the total demand for local produce is a variable quantity, it is not at all surprising that on many occasions during the survey some produce remained unsold. Clearly, over-supply was the main reason behind this. There was no widespread reduction in the prices of commodities which towards the end of a market period were certain to remain unsold, nor was produce given away. On rare occasions produce was given on credit, but from their previous experience most producers are wary of this practice. Depending mainly on its state, unsold produce is either returned home (most commonly the case), or disposed of as waste.

During the survey, the produce which consistently remained unsold was *ghola*, sweet potatoes, and bananas. *Ghola* is most tasty during the twenty-four hours or so after its removal from the oven. After that time, and weather conditions apart, the very nature of preparation – soft-cooked – renders it liable to rapid deterioration. Consequently the disposal of unsold *ghola* was inevitable. Sweet potato, on the other

[11]Regular attendance of interior villagers during the middle and end of the month did not start until 1964.

hand, has a better keeping quality than *ghola*, and, chiefly for this reason, unsold sweet potato was usually returned home. Obviously, the producer can consume it himself, but if the amount is too large, a hole dug in the ground in which the sweet potato is buried for ten to fourteen days is capable of achieving some degree of preservation. The sweet potato is then dug up again for the next market outing. This practice was followed in Tasimboko West, particularly by those living along the N̄alimbiu. There, thirty baskets of sweet potato were returned after the mid-June market (Table IV. 15); they were preserved in this fashion and sold (in new baskets, of course) at the end of June. The bulk of unsold sweet potato from Tasimboko West belonged to

Table IV. 15 Root crops offered in Honiara market by vendors from each group within Tasimboko West remaining unsold after each market period

Market period	Malaitans	Gilutae-Gaimali	Nalimbiu	Koli Point	Metepono	Roroni	Total unsold (baskets)	Total offered (baskets)	% unsold
End March	—	—	—	—	10	—	10	498	2·01
Mid-April	—	2	—	—	—	—	2	329	0·61
End April	—	4	5	—	—	—	9	707	1·27
Mid-May	—	—	—	—	—	—	—	400	—
End May	3	4	—	—	—	—	7	660	1·06
Mid-June	11	9	30	—	9	—	59	494	11·94
End June	—	2	2	—	25	15	44	660	6·67
Mid-July	—	—	—	—	—	—	—	379	—
End July	—	26	23	11	3	28	91	758	12·01
Mid-August	—	—	—	—	—	—	—	356	—
Total baskets	14	47	60	11	47	43	222	5,241	4·24

the land owners themselves, and very little of it belonged to the Malaitan migrants of Ravu, Taraia, and Susui. Several factors lie behind this. During the course of the survey and garden study it became apparent that the sweet potato fruits supplied by Malaitan migrants were much bigger than those offered by other producers. This is a direct result of their cultivation techniques: the already inherently fertile alluvium is thoroughly tilled after clearing and the well-loosened soils of the sweet potato mounds, larger and higher than those found elsewhere in Guadalcanal, cannot fail to produce heavy yields per acre. It became apparent, too, as the market survey progressed, that on the whole the Malaitans' baskets were much bigger than those of the other vendors. The most provocative demonstration of this selling practice came at the end of July when Stefanus Mirando of Susui sold in less than two hours thirteen baskets of sweet potato, each weighing well over 120 pounds, at the usual price – $1 per basket. This attracted stern looks from many producers, but no doubt delighted the fortunate buyers. But Mirando was not purposely antagonising other sellers. July 1966 was a very dry month.[12] The sweet potatoes he sold, already adversely affected by the dry spell, were not quite ready for harvesting; but rather than lose the whole crop, he harvested it and was prepared to receive less money than usual. To him bulk and low quality balanced each other, and together offset the low price received. Thus Mirando acted rationally in the light of problems which were facing him. This successful attempt to avoid a total loss is plausible when one considers that total demand for a particular commodity is unknown. Knowledge of what consumers bought on a particular previous occasion serves counsel on what and how much to produce for the next outing; this information is passed on by word of mouth, and is a hopelessly unreliable indicator of demand.

Within the context of unsold root crops, it is significant to note that during the whole survey not a single basket of yam, *panna*, or taro remained unsold. This indicates the high regard in which these tubers are held both as items of diet and for their high keeping quality, particularly yam and *panna*. Large quantities of yam reached the market-place fairly early during the end-of-May market period. But as some vendors were beginning to return home, 109 baskets of yam, averaging about 60 pounds each, arrived from Tenahulu. Many vendors thought that the Tenahulu faced the unpleasant and expensive prospect of having to return home with little produce sold. These expectations were proved wrong, for every single basket was sold during the following three days. And the Tenahulu certainly needed the money for the feast held in their village on Saturday, 8 August 1966, which was the main motive for their belated attendance on this occasion.

Unsold bananas, especially green bananas, presented little difficulty to the producer. They could either be consumed or kept until the next market outing to be offered again as ripe bananas. In this form sale is certain, since this is a commodity which is always in short supply in Honiara. Unsold vegetables, both introduced and indigenous, also presented little difficulty; if they were not disposed of as waste they were taken home where they could be consumed.

Prices

Ten cents is the basic unit of all transactions in Honiara market. All produce is sold in lots of 10 cents or multiples of 10 cents, and the use of this amount as the basic unit is convenient. It speeds up the trans-

[12]Only 128 points of rain were recorded at the Ilu Rice Experiments during that month; of this total 15 points were recorded for 4 and 5 July, while the remainder was recorded during the three days 26 to 28 July (Department of Agriculture, Honiara).

actions and helps the producer to make a quick and accurate estimate of his probable net taking and, significantly, the uses to which it might be put.

Nearly all roots were sold in $1 baskets markedly different in size so that prices varied between 1 cent per pound for Aola producers and Malaitan migrants, and 1·6 cents per pound for other producers – about half the Administration's buying price. But many Visale vendors sold roots, sweet potatoes in particular, in small 10 cent heaps ranging in weight between 3 and 5 pounds. Often an individual's heaps would not together be the equivalent of a one-dollar-worth basket from Tasimboko and other areas. By selling roots in this way, and while still adhering to the basic unit of sale (10 cents), Visale vendors manage to dispose of a smaller quantity of produce at a higher price than many other sellers, and at the same time meet the demand of buyers who do not wish to buy roots by the basket, particularly the non-Melanesian consumers. This wide variation in price per unit sold applied most commonly to fruits, especially watermelon, pineapple, and pawpaw. A fruit at 10 cents and a fruit at 20 cents might differ by as much as 6 pounds by weight while a fruit at 30 cents would be only 2 pounds heavier than the one at 20 cents. Prices therefore were determined by a rough estimation of size and by what the seller considered to be sufficient for 10 cents and multiples thereof. Once a price was set for a particular quantity of produce, either before or after the producer reached the market, little attempt was made to alter it. Only Chinese buyers and some Malaitan women tried to bargain for a reduction in price, but were never successful. A few sellers from Visale who dealt in tomatoes, lettuce, cucumber, and other easily manipulated garden produce adjusted price and quantity in response to the demand. Though not yet widespread, this practice is likely to increase as producers become more aware of changing demands.

Although the basic unit of all transactions has remained unchanged, prices have increased with the general rise in living costs during the last decade. Honiara market is no exception in this respect. The price of fowl has risen by 100 per cent since 1957, from 50 cents to $1; roots which were once obtained at 8 pounds for 10 cents are now offering at about half the amount for the same price; while eight coconuts used to be offered for 10 cents, now only three coconuts (either ripe or green) can be bought with the same amount of money.

To an outside observer, and particularly to many non-indigenous buyers, the large majority of sellers appear not at all eager to sell their produce. This is an interpretation of indigenous behaviour based on outside norms. Producers lay out their wares for prospective buyers to inspect and choose according to their requirements. Producers from the same area normally come together and tend to form a group, although they do not monopolise particular sectors of the market. Each member of the group has some idea of what his neighbour has to offer. Invariably the group is tied together by residence, social and interpersonal relations. Any member of the group can and will collect the purchase money from the buyer if the owner is not close at hand. Producers consider that after the produce is arranged there is no need for further advertisement, which would run counter to the traditional concept of reciprocity and exchange with certain chosen partners. And in the new situation, producers consider it proper that prospective buyers should be unfettered in their choice of 'partners' and their produce. The transaction is highly impersonal, but this traditional attitude prevails as an undercurrent among producers. Despite these behavioural restraints, however, there is a real anxiety to make a sale.

The main sources of market income

A seller's net income from a market outing depends on three main factors: the type or types of produce offered, the volume actually disposed through sale, and the fare and freight structure levied by the truck or launch owner-operator. Fare and freight rates will be discussed later; here it is sufficient to remark that for the same distance they vary a great deal both between different carriers and between different dates. These comments should be borne in mind as a general framework within which the following analysis of the income patterns of sellers from different areas is made.

It is clear from the pattern of supply of foodstuffs that some classes of produce are more significant than others as major income-earners, while some produce classes are more significant in certain areas, to the extent that some degree of specialisation arises. The end-of-June survey material has been analysed and tabulated to illustrate this point (Table IV. 16). It is apparent that roots were the major earners of cash for the majority of producers, with Tasimboko West clearly prominent. Bearing in mind the dominant role of roots during the whole survey, it seems certain that roots provided the main source of income to the overwhelming majority of vendors. The importance of roots to the Tasimboko and Malaitans west of the Balesuna cannot be over-emphasised. A similar position prevailed in Tasimboko East, although there the proportion of sellers depending on roots was not as high as west of the Balesuna, and in contrast to it, traditional stimulants, betel particularly, commanded a significant place as a main money-earner. In Visale, sellers relied for their market income on a much wider range of produce, although roots still remained the major source of cash to the majority. Not surprisingly, 'European' vegetables appeared as the major source of cash to some vendors from that area only. The dependence of some

Visale sellers on vegetables was matched by Paripao's role as sole supplier of articles of native manufacture reaching the Honiara market. Both classes of produce are normally not bulky, but the latter's contributions are usually more remunerative for each unit of quantity sold. For Nggela suppliers, cooked foods and uncooked meat and fish were the main sources of income.

Incomes from market outings

The results of income analysis in terms of average total income per producer during the whole survey, the average income at each date of the survey together with standard deviations from the means for those dates for the main areas represented, reveal some interesting facts (Table IV. 17). At a district level, Nggela was the only area for which the average total income was substantially more than half the figure for Tasimboko West, while Visale and Paripao totals were less than half the figure for Nggela. Nggela's high placing was the result of the sale of large quantities of both cooked foods and uncooked meat and fish, items with an unsatisfied demand amongst Honiara's Melanesian consumers.

Within Tasimboko West itself, only the Malaitan migrants, the locals on both sides of the N̄alimbiu, and the Gilutae-Gaimali group had average total incomes in excess of the district average. But this district average sinks into relative insignificance when placed against the Malaitans'; indeed the earnings of this group are the main element in the region's high average total income, in comparison to those of other districts. Only the figure for the N̄alimbiu group exceeds half the Malaitans' total.

Average incomes during each of the survey dates re-emphasise the prominence of the Malaitan migrants, particularly on six of the ten survey dates. On several of those six occasions, the average incomes of Malaitan migrants were as much as two to three times, in some cases four times, those of other areas taken individually, both inside Tasimboko and outside it. The exceptions were the two surveys during May, and those of mid-July and mid-August. On those occasions only the figures for Metepono and Koli Point (during May), N̄alimbiu (mid-July and mid-August) and Malango (mid-August) exceeded those for the Malaitans. The reasons for this are not far to seek. At the mid-May survey only one producer came from the Metepono area and sold vast quantities of roots, while the four producers from Koli Point between them disposed of more than fifty dollars' worth of produce. At the end-of-May survey, three Metepono producers contributed the bulk of the hundred and fifty dollars' worth of watermelon sold; their average income was the highest for any date during the survey, exclud-

Table IV. 16 Percentage classification of income derived in Honiara market at the end-of-June market period*

		Malaitans	Tasimboko West	Tasimboko East	Paripao	Malango	Visale	Nggela	Total	%
Roots	$	17	61	23	4	6	34	—	145	67·44
	%	94·44	82·43	53·49	33·34	85·71	59·64	—		
Fruits	$	1	4	1	1	—	5	—	12	5·58
	%	5·56	5·41	2·33	8·33	—	8·77	—		
Cooked foods	$		4	5	—	—	6	1	16	7·44
	%		5·41	11·63	—	—	10·53	25·00		
Uncooked foods	$		5	2	1	1	2	3	14	6·51
	%		6·75	4·65	8·33	14·29	3·51	75·00		
Coconuts	$	—	—	3	—	—	2	—	5	2·32
	%	—	—	6·97	—	—	3·51	—		
Traditional stimulants	$	—	—	9	3	—	6	—	18	8·37
	%	—	—	20·93	25·00	—	10·53	—		
Handicrafts	$	—	—	—	3	—	—	—	3	1·39
	%	—	—	—	25·00	—	—	—		
European vegetables	$	—	—	—	—	—	2	—	2	0·94
	%	—	—	—	—	—	3·51			
Total income	$	18	74	43	12	7	57	4	215	100

*Reading down: income derived by vendors of each District and by Malaitans from Tasimboko West from sale of produce within each produce class.

Reading across: income derived from sale of produce within each produce class by vendors from each District and by Malaitans from Tasimboko West.

Table IV. 17 Mean income (with standard deviations) derived from Honiara market by vendors of each District, and from each group within Tasimboko West, at each market period

Area/District		End Mar. ($)	Mid-Apr. ($)	End Apr. ($)	Mid-May ($)	End May ($)	Mid-June ($)	End June ($)	Mid-July ($)	End July ($)	Mid-Aug. ($)	Average over whole period ($)
Malaitans	1	15.54	23.28	20.80	8.67	15.08	13.19	13.35	13.27	12.29	10.47	55.63
	2	12.17	12.66	15.40	8.47	15.36	9.76	9.95	13.93	11.69	10.89	
Gilutae-	1	8.49	5.98	8.76	7.75	7.10	8.74	6.20	6.84	4.30	3.95	23.03
Gaimali	2	5.29	2.71	8.49	4.68	7.35	7.08	4.21	4.17	2.69	2.58	
N̄alimbiu	1	9.12	8.00	14.42	7.14	13.00	8.15	9.00	19.94	6.90	14.53	27.84
	2	4.95	9.32	10.60	2.76	9.21	4.78	8.95	17.08	5.92	6.20	
Koli Point	1	5.58	6.39	7.20	11.87	4.29	5.77	6.60	—	6.36	2.40	12.52
	2	2.18	1.17	4.25	9.96	2.62	2.79	1.47	—	4.70	—	
Metepono	1	8.33	2.80	12.90	32.54	20.57	3.35	5.12	6.15	4.82	3.22	11.44
	2	7.38	1.43	3.20	—	26.24	1.08	4.90	4.03	3.92	3.44	
Tenahulu	1	3.80	—	—	—	9.28	—	—	—	—	—	9.60
	2	—	—	—	—	8.52	—	—	—	—	—	
Gorabau	1	5.54	5.25	4.58	1.35	6.51	3.80	7.22	7.07	2.81	3.59	11.51
	2	1.77	2.05	3.78	—	3.11	—	1.28	3.86	1.59	1.84	
Suagi	1	4.80	7.11	2.53	8.50	3.91	—	2.85	4.92	5.66	3.35	6.43
	2	—	3.37	2.16	—	3.74	—	3.24	1.89	2.57	1.83	
Roroni	1	1.10	—	3.47	3.80	4.86	4.70	3.88	5.41	5.20	5.88	9.63
	2	0.25	—	1.80	3.93	3.71	2.61	2.83	3.22	3.63	1.55	
	2	8.25	8.99	9.58	8.49	8.88	8.05	6.89	9.60	6.18	5.98	19.41
Tasimboko West	1	6.88	9.04	10.36	7.59	11.43	7.03	6.99	10.85	6.24	6.24	
Aola	1	8.97	—	6.40	6.45	—	—	—	—	—	—	7.26
	2	11.14	—	3.63	5.59	—	—	—	—	—	—	
Malango	1	3.65	2.60	2.50	4.97	2.53	—	5.31	1.96	8.05	12.96	7.71
	2	2.73	0.20	—	3.38	2.69	—	9.77	1.98	4.03	9.14	
Tasimboko East	1	5.78	21.00	4.23	12.80	5.55	3.43	4.55	3.20	4.03	—	7.07
	2	5.86	—	2.80	—	4.04	1.67	4.79	1.98	3.38	—	
Paripao	1	3.16	—	2.28	—	2.91	—	3.11	—	3.11	—	3.93
	2	3.27	—	1.25	—	0.24	—	1.63	—	0.20	—	
Visale	1	4.13	4.26	4.63	3.63	4.23	3.74	4.67	4.61	2.10	3.44	6.01
	2	1.91	3.11	2.96	3.01	3.53	2.24	3.38	2.45	1.73	2.60	
Nggela	1	—	—	15.60	—	52.00	—	3.10	—	—	—	13.33
	2	—	—	—	—	—	—	1.99	—	—	—	

1 Mean. 2 Standard deviation.

ing the unusual figure for mid-May. The same factors are applicable in the dominance of the N̄alimbiu area at the mid-July and mid-August surveys.

Outside Tasimboko West, Malango's average income alone rose above the Malaitans', and only on one occasion (mid-August). There, too, a small number of producers, three in this case, earned between them nearly forty dollars, one of them $25.40 for the sale of a dug-out canoe to a previously arranged Malaitan customer, resident in Honiara.

The average incomes for Aola, Paripao, and Visale need some comment and clarification. Aola was represented only three times during the entire survey; nearly all sellers from that area attended only once. But during those periods individual incomes were, on the whole, high. Much of the Aola's earning was by way of roots and uncooked meat and fish; it contributed more than 8 per cent of all roots supplied on each of the three dates it was represented, and 80 per cent of all the uncooked meat and fish, fowl especially, at the mid-May survey. With only infrequent and costly sea transport available, Aola producers must offer produce in quantity and at a high price per unit of quantity. The same principle applies for Paripao, but with one significant additional handicap. This is the limitation placed by distance and weight on what an individual can carry from his village, invariably over rough country, to Roroni, whence the remainder of the journey to Honiara is by truck. Paripao producers did bring high-cost produce for sale, but many could not bring a sufficiently large quantity to give them a net income above $5. In fact, during the whole survey only one person from Paripao earned more than this amount and only on one occasion, through the sale of betel. Visale average income per survey ranged between $2.10 at the end of July and $4.67 at the end of June. These comparatively low figures result chiefly from attendance of large numbers of sellers with produce which netted individual incomes well below $10.00. Individual incomes in excess of this value were earned by only fourteen different Visale sellers throughout the entire survey, but not one of these men earned up to $16.00 per market trip. This is quite contrary to Tasimboko experience.

Absence of large individual incomes at Visale is shown by comparatively low standard deviations throughout the period. Moreover, the difference between highest and lowest standard deviations is the least for any area – evidence of a constantly low departure from the mean of individual incomes throughout the survey. For Tasimboko West, on the other hand, a number of individual incomes of $50 and more give sufficient weight to the total income to endure both a high average individual income per outing and high standard deviations for the whole of Tasimboko West, and most especially the Malaitan migrants. At the end of June, for instance, 7 per cent of Tasimboko West vendors earned incomes more than two standard deviations from the area's high mean for that month ($6.89), while 8 per cent from Visale earned incomes of that order (with their low mean $4.67 and low standard deviation $3.38) during that period.

But how profitable is the sale of produce in Honiara market in terms of total cash receipts, and in comparison with other sources of income? Six specific cases are taken to illustrate the position; the cash earnings from all sources of these individuals for the period April-July inclusive are used (Table IV. 18). Stefanus Mirando and Are Vakaia represent the Malaitan migrants in Tasimboko West. The former is a non-rent-paying tenant-at-will of the government at Susui, while the latter is dependent on a Tasimboko landlord at Ravu. Stefanus represents the peak of financial success in Malaitan participation in the sale of foodstuffs in the Honiara market, while Are typifies their average position. But both attended the market at all dates. Silas Bosule of Gaimali

Table IV. 18 Sources of cash earnings of selected individuals in Tasimboko West, April-July 1966

Name	Place of residence	Home District	Honiara market	Copra sales	Wage employment and employer	Total income
Stefanus Mirando	Susui	Malaita	$286.85	—	Agr. Dept (contract) $4.50	$291.35
Are Vakaia	Ravu	Malaita	$125.40	—	—	$125.40
Silas Bosule	Gaimali	Gorabau	$95.35	—	—	$95.35
Robert Rava	Tasimboko	Tasimboko	$19.65	$184.54*	—	$204.19
Solomon Biga	Abuabili	Tasimboko	—	—	Tenaru Timber Co. $102.34	$102.34
Daniel Buto	Honiara	Roroni Tasimboko	—	—	Clerk Lands Dept $184.00	$184.00

*May to August copra income used, to give a length of time comparable with the others.

village represents those Tasimboko for whom sale of produce was the main source of cash income during the course of the survey. No bearing coconut groves were under his direct control, neither did he gain access to any through customary means during the period of study. He, too, attended every market. Robert Rava of Gorabau village, with a market attendance rate of 40 per cent, almost double the average rate for his village, here represents those Tasimboko for whom sale of local produce in Honiara market is not the main source of cash income. He is in control of more than twenty-five acres of bearing coconut palms –

obviously his main source of cash. Solomon Biga of Abuabili and Daniel Buto of Roroni represent the Tasimboko in permanent cash employment, the former in the rural area, the latter in the town and with considerable potential opportunities for advancement.

A comparison of the incomes earned by these selected individuals (Table IV. 18) reveals clearly that under present conditions sale of foodstuffs in the Honiara market is rewarding to the Tasimboko and Malaitan migrant prepared to make the necessary effort. Indeed, it can be as or more rewarding than unskilled wage labour, in Tasimboko itself or in Honiara. But to the Tasimboko in command of other cash-yielding resources, coconuts in particular, the need to earn money is not the primary reason behind a market outing. The purpose is rather to spend money earned from copra sales, and the opportunity is afforded by the availability of transport at market times. Some surplus ripe coconuts and roots are usually taken along to offset the higher fares one would have to pay as a passenger with no accompanying cargoes.

The Malaitans

An obvious query demands reply here: why do the Malaitan migrants hold such a prominent place as suppliers of produce in the Honiara market? One obvious reason needs re-emphasising. Opportunities for wage labour in non-Melanesian enterprises inside Tasimboko West have stabilised, following promulgation of the new Labour Regulation early in 1960 and abolition of the system of recruiting workers for a definite contract period. Workers are staying longer at their jobs. Employment opportunities provided by Tasimboko entrepreneurs are very limited, and definitely less rewarding financially than work for expatriates. Further, recent Malaitan migrants lack facilities available to those longer-term residents who have married local women, associated with local big men for considerable lengths of time, and who have acquired access to resources like coconuts. Recent arrivals have been allocated only unused forest-covered soils, and can earn money only from quick maturing crops.

Not so obvious, however, are the sets of interpersonal relationships which give a delicate and uncertain foundation to the agricultural and produce-marketing operations of most Malaitan migrants. This precarious base offers little security. Obligations arbitrarily attached to land grants by the land-holder are not matters for negotiation or bargain. The grantor extends limited usage rights; the grantee accepts without question and indeed cannot afford to do otherwise. As with the Indians in Fiji, uncertain land tenure seems to sharpen the motive to make short-term profits.

The Malaitans at Susui have a particular problem. In 1964 the government leased the land on which they were living from the Tasimboko owners. The change in landlord has not resulted in brighter prospects. Now they have the minimum of contact with an impersonal landlord who tolerates their presence since much ground is being cleared of its dense forest cover in the course of gardening activities, thus reducing considerably the cost of clearing should the area be developed for large-scale mechanised agriculture. From the government's point of view, these Malaitans provide a ready source of labour should major clearing and other work be undertaken on the N̄alimbiu irrigation canal. The Administration has discouraged these migrants from planting permanent cash crops, and, should government succeed in attracting developers into the area, they should be ready to vacate it.

Uncertainty for the future is thus the dominant and uniting factor in the lot of the recently settled Malaitan migrants in Tasimboko West. There are instances, as at Ravu, where Malaitans are planting coconuts for the Tasimboko land owner, and here the Malaitans themselves bring closer the time when they must consider other means of earning money. But while this moment is still some distance away, they make the most of the current situation and play a leading role in the provision of local staples for sale in the Honiara market.

The uncertainty of transport arrangements

The general lack of a regular means of transport, distance from Honiara, desire to reach the market as near as possible to the mid-month or end-of-month pay-days, plus the degree of preparation needed, seem to be the major variables behind the actual choice of time at which preparation for a market outing is commenced. The two to three days before the middle and end of a month, often more, are times of intensive preparation by vendors. Depending chiefly on the nature of the produce to be sold, and other commitments close to or during those pre-market days, this preparation involves the whole family; *ghola*-making is normally a female chore, while sweet potato-pulling is done by both sexes. It is only common sense that producers be ready with their produce before the carrier arrives, but it is not so immediately apparent that in his choice of time and day to commence preparations, the producer is involved in no small degree of risk-taking. Even if the producer had previously given notice to the carrier of intention to be ready at a certain date, carriers themselves are few in number, with varied commitments, leading to possible delays. The producer may have to wait for some time, with consequent deterioration of produce, before his need can be met. In the present circumstances in the Solomons, such risks are inevitable and universal, though they vary in degree of gravity. In the long view, the sooner producers come to grips fully with such market forces, the sooner they too might make the appropriate wide-ranging adjustments to them. Indeed, the Tasimboko west of the Balesuna have made an attempt at co-operative organisation in the Gaubata Development Society (unregistered), the marketing activities of which commenced at the end of November 1966, well after and outside the scope of this survey.

The risk of produce deterioration and the difficulty of securing transport facilities vary in direct proportion to distance from Honiara, irrespective of the causes of these difficulties and the precise means of transport available. For the Aola, for example, sea transport is and will remain the most feasible means of transporting produce to Honiara for at least the next ten to fifteen years.[13] It is not uncommon for Aola producers to send notice to the carriers a week or more before the actual date and make the necessary preparation three to four days before the market day. Their produce, roots especially, has deteriorated somewhat by the time it reaches the market, but generally early arrival and demand for roots in Honiara result in a quick and ready sale of produce.

The cost of transport

Aola. The joy and satisfaction derived from an early sale of somewhat deteriorated produce must be muted by transport costs (Table IV. 19). For the three dates on which Aola vendors were present, a total of $112.45 was paid for freight on goods and passenger fares. This was made up by a charge of 20 cents per basket of sweet potatoes and other produce the value of which was $1 per unit sold, while adult passengers, with or without cargoes, paid 60 cents per head each way and minors travelled at half rate. The figures speak for themselves, particularly the average cost per person per outing and the actual cost of marketing to this particular group of producers. Transport claimed more than one-third of the group's gross income.

It is not possible to say how much of the charge for carriage is clear profit to the carrier. But on these three occasions, when the launch and cutter concerned each shipped into Honiara no less than twenty-five bags of copra along with Aola produce, and made trips to Nggela and Savo while the Aola people sold their goods in Honiara, it seems certain that fare and freight charges on produce provided a most valuable

[13]Appendix II of the White Paper on Roads Policy (BSIP 1966:24) places the Roroni-Aola road as second in priority for Guadalcanal, but fourth for the entire Solomons. During 1966 road construction work on Guadalcanal concentrated on the Naro-Lambi Bay stretch, and the road engineer responsible for Guadalcanal expressed the view that the Roroni-Aola road is not likely to be considered during the next five years. Now the Metepono bridge has to be reconstructed before a move further east can be made, thus delaying further the consideration of the Roroni-Aola road, and even then other unforeseeable factors, of which finance is the most important, may cause still further delays.

source of income, and, in the case of the *Koli*, sufficient to meet almost half the total running costs per month, without depreciation and other charges.[14]

The high cost of transport is primarily the result of the method of assessing the freight charged on the volume of goods carried. For Aola, it works at approximately $1.67 per ton mile. Given such a high freight rate, it is obvious that each market vendor needs to carry a large volume of goods if his net income is not to be insignificant after paying the carrier.

Koli Point-Gilutae. The same general principle applies to the Tasimboko west from Koli Point. These groups of sellers have established a firm association with a particular carrier (Table IV. 19), who charges them (at the rate of 15 cents per basket of produce worth $1 over fifteen miles) on an average, $3.70 per ton mile – 122 per cent over the Aola rate. However, average transport cost per seller is only 47 per cent of the high Aola figure. The number of Tasimboko vendors who depended on Leong Hang for transport to Honiara averaged thirty-two throughout this market study. This ensured a relatively low average cost per vendor per outing. Aola sellers averaged ten persons per outing. The result was a much higher average cost per vendor per market trip.

Gorabau-Suagi. The reliance of the Tasimboko west from Koli Point on Leong Hang for produce marketing is matched by the reliance of the two villages of Gorabau and Suagi on Lo See War (Table IV. 19). Total transport costs per market for these two villages are much lower than those for the two localities noted above. This is due in the main to the fact that the sale of produce in Honiara market, small as it is in total value, is only a convenient but subsidiary activity in those villages; copra bought by the same trader is their main source of cash. The freight rate per basket of produce worth $1 is the same as for Leong Hang. The distance covered by Lo See War (25 miles) on the forward journey, however, is nearly double that travelled by Leong Hang (15 miles) on a single trip to haul the produce of vendors in the Koli Point-Gilutae area. The effect is an average freight cost of $2.20 per ton mile, which falls between those for Aola and Tasimboko west from Koli Point.

Susui Malaitans. The Malaitans at Susui dealt with three separate carriers during this survey. At the March and mid-April markets, they used a land-rover and trailer made available by the Department of Agriculture field officer responsible for rice experiments at Ilu. No transport costs were paid on these occasions and they received the full

[14]The *Koli* consumes up to twenty-four dollars' worth of diesel fuel per month and wages for its four crew members amount to $55: at total of $79 per month running expenses. This launch belongs to Samuel Saki of Koli village.

Table IV. 19 Analysis of the cost of transport to Honiara market in 1966 for various groups of vendors from areas east of Honiara

Locality	Carrier	Distance covered on all trips (miles)	Total number of vendors	Total cost to all vendors combined ($)	Transport cost as % of gross income	Av. cost per seller ($)	Av. cost per seller per mile (cents)
Aola	*Koli* & *Fairwind* (launch & cutter)	270	30	112.45			
Av. per market		90	10	37.48	35·72	3.74	4
Koli Point–Gilutae	Leong Hang	645	327	518.51			
Av. per market		64·5	32·7	51.85	18·54	1.76	2·8
Gorabau–Suagi	Lo See War	450	128	134.49			
Av. per market		50	14·2	15.05	15·73	1.11	2·2
Susui Malaitans	C.C.A.	28	8	13.25			
Av. per market		14	4	6.62	11·40	1.65	11
Susui Malaitans	Lo See War	84	40	58.50			
Av. per market		14	6·6	8.41	12·38	1.46	10
Taraia Malaitans	Mahabir	162	1	54.00			
Av. per market		18		6.00	16·35	6.00	33

value of their produce. At the end of April and end of July, the Malaitans used the Central Co-operative Association's (C.C.A.) truck. The C.C.A. charged 25 cents per mile covered, plus 50 cents per hour taken to collect the produce and dispose of it in Honiara. At these rates, the Malaitans paid the C.C.A. an average of $1.65 per seller per visit (Table IV. 19). The C.C.A. truck carted about 4·5 tons of produce on those two occasions for a total cost of $13.25, over a distance of fourteen miles each time. This works out at about 30 cents per ton mile.

During the other six market periods, the Malaitans hired Lo See War's truck. On these occasions, forty vendors each paid an average of $1.46 per trip. The truck carried more than fifteen tons of produce, for which Lo See War received over $58. This is the equivalent of about 27 cents per ton mile. It is in marked contrast to the rate the same carrier charged Suagi and Gorabau vendors. When dealing with the Tasimboko, Lo See War places a charge on individual units of produce valued at $1. For the Malaitans, an initial flat rate of $8 per fourteen-mile trip is levied; excess charge is arbitrarily added to this minimum figure after making a rough assessment of the probable total value of the produce carried. This system of assessing the cost of transport allows room for wide fluctuations in the actual amounts paid by the vendors from time to time. However, cost per ton mile is much lower than that paid by the Tasimboko.

Taraia Malaitans. Unlike the Susui migrants, those at Taraia have established a link with a particular Fiji-Indian truck operator: B. Mahabir, a senior mechanic with the Public Works Department. Mahabir purchased second-hand from the British Solomon Islands Trading Corporation a vehicle capable of carrying up to forty baskets of sweet potatoes. He levies a flat rate of $6 per load, irrespective of the volume of goods carried, for all places about the N̄alimbiu River. On the nine occasions the Taraia Malaitans came to market, more than nine tons of produce were hauled for them by Mahabir. On the basis of these figures, the average rate per ton mile – 33 cents – is similar to those paid by their 'one talk' at Susui to the C.C.A. and Lo See War.

An additional point to note concerning Mahabir's operations east of Honiara is that this low rate of freight per ton mile is levied on all producers east of the capital. However, very few Tasimboko West vendors hired Mahabir's truck during this survey. Many of his clients east of the town were from Tasimboko East; this was due mainly to the arrangements made by one of his drivers, who comes from that Sub-district.

Visale. Three carriers participate regularly in the hauling of produce from Visale to the Honiara market. These are Mahabir, Chottu, and Baruno. Like Mahabir, Baruno also carts produce from east of

Honiara, while Chottu's transport activities are largely confined to Visale producers.

It is likely that Baruno and Chottu have a slight initial advantage over Mahabir in the Visale produce transporting business. Baruno is a local man; he comes from Kakambona, the peri-urban village west of Honiara. His enterprise is the culmination of a long period of capital accumulation; his savings were earned from the sale of garden produce to Honiara's urban population. Baruno's truck can carry up to thirty baskets of sweet potatoes. Chottu is Mahabir's countryman, and, like him, works as a mechanic with the Public Works Department. But he has married a Visale woman and is therefore better known by the people of that area. On many occasions Mrs Chottu actually organised the market trips. Chottu's truck, bought second-hand from the Medical Department in 1964, has a carrying capacity of approximately one and a half tons.

These three carriers use the same method of freight computation; their freight rates vary with distance travelled. Both Mahabir and Baruno charge $7 for a journey from the Visale Lighthouse to Honiara (21 miles); the rate increases to $8 as far as Maravovo (25 miles). This works out at approximately 29 cents per ton mile for both carriers. Baruno uses the same rate when hauling Tasimboko produce, while Mahabir's freight rate for that area is slightly higher. Because of a greater carrying capacity, Chottu's actual charges for distances travelled are slightly higher than those of Baruno and Mahabir, but his rates per ton mile – 18 cents for Visale and 21 cents for Tasimboko – are the lowest for any carrier during the survey.

Despite the apparent relative advantages of Chottu and Baruno over Mahabir in the Visale transport business, sellers from that area do not patronise a particular carrier. They will travel on the first truck available to them. Thus some degree of competition among these three carriers is apparent. It would seem that this is the main factor in the lower rates prevailing there, in comparison with those paid by vendors coming from Tasimboko and beyond. Competition among carriers operating east of Honiara is virtually impossible, since vendors from that general area patronise particular carriers. Although Baruno, Chottu, and Mahabir provide alternative means of transport to the people east of the capital, the attraction provided by their comparatively lower freight rates does not weaken the transport monopoly already established there by Leong Hang and Lo See War.

Cost to the carrier. But how profitable are these transport operations from the viewpoint of the carriers themselves? In the case of the *Koli*, the Aola vendors pay in transport costs sufficient to meet up to one-half that launch's ordinary running expenses per month – no mean contribution to that enterprise as an economic venture. Mahabir's case will give some idea of the economics of transporting produce under both Visale and Tasimboko West conditions. This operator earned on an average a gross income of $150 per month. His ordinary runninng expenses, including the drivers' wages, did not exceed $70 in any one month. Maintenance was done at little or no financial cost. The vehicle was bought for $500 in 1964; depreciation at the rate of at least 30 per cent per year would have reduced its value to about $245 in 1966. This works out to a monthly depreciation rate of about $6. The annual registration fee (without insurance) would come to about $2.50 per month. Allowing about $20 per month for unexpected expenditure, total expenses to this particular operator would come to about $98.50 per month. This gives a probable net income of at least $50 per month, of which up to one-third would be derived from the operations of the middle- and end-of-month markets. Chottu's position is similar, although for him the figures themselves would be higher because of larger carrying capacity and greater running costs.

From Asian-trader monopoly to the emergence of Melanesian enterprise

Thus it is clear that the transport of produce is entirely outside the control of producers themselves. 'Professional' carriers have emerged following the extension of road construction.

Transport costs vary widely among carriers and for a single carrier. Although some competition among hauliers is apparent, standing arrangements between producers and particular carriers are still prevalent. At the same time, the greater share of the financial benefits is received by non-Melanesians, although Melanesian carriers offer other alternatives. At the end of November 1966 the Tasimboko between Roroni and Gilutae secured a tractor and trailer specifically for carting produce into Honiara. This was made possible with the assistance of a loan from the Agricultural and Industrial Loans Board to supplement their own accumulated funds. Although it is too early to judge its operation, it is clear that many producers in the area have ceased to cart produce through the Chinese traders and have turned to their own vehicle for transport. This is a promising sign, and, given proper management (admittedly a big requirement under local conditions), should be of tremendous value to the Tasimboko people and may eventually reduce considerably the volume of goods hauled by non-Melanesians.

Conclusion

Honiara market owes its origin to Agricultural Department attempts to dispose of its surplus roots and vegetables after it had satisfied the requirements of certain government departments. This was a small beginning, and at times was insufficient to meet the needs of the town population not receiving ration issues from the Administration.

The change of control at Ilu in 1955 and the diversification of the functions of Kukum Agricultural Station provided the major opening to indigenous producers to supply vegetables and roots both to government institutions and the Honiara market itself, which came under the control of the District Administration between 1950 and 1957, and has been under the control of the Honiara Town Council ever since. But it was not until early in 1964 that regular attendance became possible from more distant areas, particularly the interior bush villages of Paripao and Malango. This is in large measure the result of road rehabilitation and bridge construction. Until that date, regular sale of produce in Honiara market was limited to those close to and with definite and reliable means of access to the town; the Visale sellers and the Tasimboko west of Koli Point were regular participants.

During the immediate post-war decade there was no urgent necessity for the Tasimboko and Visale to produce a surplus of foodstuffs for sale in Honiara; alternative means of earning cash were available. Today, Honiara has become more accessible, wage employment openings have stabilised, and the Tasimboko are responding successfully to the improved opportunity to sell local produce in Honiara. They now supply the bulk of the produce reaching the market. But from Tasimboko, Malaitan migrants play a leading role. The Tasimboko exist in the relative security of their own society and its lands; the Malaitan migrant, on the other hand, suffers uncertainty over his future, and has delicate and sometimes strained relations with the Tasimboko landlords. Malaitans therefore must produce food crops, sweet potatoes in particular, for sale in the Honiara market, if they are to meet their varied and increasing cash commitments. In financial terms, their activities as producers and sellers of local garden produce in the Honiara market tower above those of the others. Their financial gains from produce-marketing compare well with returns from unskilled wage labour both within and outside Tasimboko.

Yet whether the seller is a migrant or otherwise, a high proportion of the fruits of his labour go to the truck or cutter operator; and the most significant recipient in this respect is the non-Melanesian operator. Some Melanesians are participating in the truck business, although their number is small and share of the proceeds low. But the Gaubata Development Society, with its new tractor and trailer, has already gained the support of the majority of sellers west of the Balesuna. At the same time a group of sellers from Taboko, Visale, hire it regularly every Friday to cart their produce for the Saturday morning market. This is a hopeful progress in a field where Melanesian attempts in the past have often wandered astray, and its success is vitally significant to no less than 1,000 persons who have been committed to market production as a major source of income for the past decade.

V

Produce Marketing in a Polynesian Society: Apia, Western Samoa

B. A. Lockwood

From their first contacts with the Samoan people early in the nineteenth century European explorers, whalers, traders, and missionaries found it fairly easy to obtain goods and services from the Samoans in exchange for various 'trade goods'. The Europeans regarded this as trade – the exchange of goods and services at some mutually agreed rate of price. The Samoans could not initially have seen it this way. It was the responsibility of a Samoan to treat a visitor with the courtesy and honour due to his rank – to feed, house, and if necessary to clothe him – to attend to any requests he might make. The visitor in turn might show his appreciation for the hospitality and assistance received by presenting the host with a gift of ceremonial value, such as a finely woven pandanus cloak (*'ie toga*). On leaving his host the visitor would take with him a continuing obligation to extend hospitality to members of the host's family if they passed through his village. This form of exchange is essentially different from the European's notion of trade which involves the accounting mechanism of an exchange rate or price and which, once completed, leaves no obligation on either party to trade in the future.

In 1835 the first European missionaries landed in Samoa and shortly

My thanks go to Mr Max Cunliffe of the Department of Agriculture, Western Samoa, for his support of this study, and to my field assistant, Viliamu Brown, and the ten volunteers from the Department of Agriculture who did all the hard work in the survey. I wish to thank Mr E. K. Fisk of the Australian National University for his guidance in the preparation of this paper.

afterwards took up permanent residence in the islands. About the same time whalers began calling at a harbour on the north coast of Upolu Island, which became the headquarters of the commercial conquest of Samoa by foreigners.

> By 1860 over a hundred Europeans were permanently settled round the shores of Apia harbour, running various types of businesses – such as general stores, boarding-houses, and grog-shops – and practising a variety of trades. Others had settled on the land nearby and were producing foodstuffs for the trade with visiting ships. And still others had established themselves as traders in the outer districts. (Davidson 1967: 38)

The Samoans were soon drawn into this developing web of trade. Around Apia harbour

> some supplied foodstuffs to the merchants and to visiting ships. Some entered the employment of European residents or were engaged as sailors on local or overseas vessels. And they developed, at the same time, a demand for the manufactured goods that the merchants imported . . . Till Europeans settled there, only Apia village – from which the embryo town took its name – lay on the shores of the harbour, and a number of villages lay some distance inland. But before 1860 many of the people of these latter villages had shifted to the coast. People from more distant parts also, had begun to move in, attracted by the excitement and opportunities provided by commercial development. (Davidson 1967: 39)

From these early beginnings Apia has developed as the government and administrative capital of Western Samoa as well as continuing as the country's entrepôt. In 1961 some 21,699 persons lived in the Apia township, including most of the 668 resident Europeans and a large proportion of the part-Samoan section of the population. Most of Western Samoa's wage and salary earners work and live in or near Apia. Most of the country's commercial coconut and cacao plantations lie close to Apia along the northwest coast of Upolu. The country's bus services are Apia-oriented – all buses leave the outer villages in time to reach Apia between seven and eight in the morning. Most of them wait out the day in Apia and return to the outer villages in the late afternoon. Even the buses on Savai'i Island operate in a similar way. They travel to the inter-island ferry wharf at Salelologa so that passengers can arrive in Apia between seven and eight.

Most outer villages have trade stores which sell a variety of imported goods – food, clothing, household utensils, and work tools – and buy village produce such as copra and cacao for export. All Samoan families earn some cash income from export crops and they all use and consume imported goods and foodstuffs. Money has become useful and desirable and is acceptable in many instances as an alternative to the traditional ceremonial valuables as gifts intended to show respect, and as payment for traditional crafts such as house and canoe building. But while money is widely accepted and used, commercial trade is limited to transactions with the stores and government marketing agencies. It is limited in the main to goods which enter international trade, Samoan exports and imports of foreign goods. Exchanges between Samoans are still based predominantly on the traditional system of reciprocity. Each village still produces the bulk of its food and housing needs, and there is little difference between villages in the types of commodities and services produced for their own consumption and use.

Trade in village-produced commodities has not developed between the villages or between families in a village. Temporary shortages in a family or in a whole village are met by neighbouring families or villages as a matter of course. The receiving family or village at one time may be the giving family or village at another. It is very difficult for a Samoan to refuse a request for something he has even if, by giving it, he will himself be short or have to go without. Many Apia residents maintain close family relationships in the outer villages. Some hold chiefly titles as heads of outer village families. These connections, some based on reciprocal obligations built up over time, and others based on the responsibility to serve and support a family chief, have kept up a flow of village-produced food to Apia outside the trade sector of the economy.

Some food is produced in the villages which make up the Apia township. Even in the new 'suburban' housing settlements such as that at Vaivase, breadfruit, bananas, taro, and *ta'amu*[1] are grown on the house blocks. The banana export trade indirectly provides another source of staple food; bananas packed for export in the villages are inspected in Apia before being shipped and rejected fruit is sold in Apia. In most Apia families imported foods such as rice and flour (and bread) have become acceptable substitutes for the Samoan staples. The Apia stores have not, however, made any effort to provide Samoan staple foods for sale. It seems that until recent years Apia residents have been adequately provided with food through the arrangements described. Most of the Samoan staple food had entered Apia through channels other than that of commercial trade. This supply pattern still operates but in recent years an outdoor market has developed in Apia which has altered the pattern significantly and has cut across the traditional

[1]A number of Samoan commodity names are used in this paper. They are: *'ava* – kava, root of the plant *Piper methysticum*, from which the ceremonial drink *'ava* is prepared; *laufala (puono)* and *laupuona* – dried leaves of two varieties of pandanus used for weaving mats; *limu* – seaweed; *lu'au* – bundles of taro leaves; *pola* – plaited coconut leaf blind; *salu* – Samoan broom made from coconut leaf mid-ribs; *sea* – the inside of a mollusc; *ta'amu* – a food plant, the stem of which looks and tastes rather like taro when cooked *(Alocasia* sp.*)*; *tauaga* – bundles of plantain fibres used as a strainer; *'ula* – various necklaces or garlands of seeds or flowers, etc.; *vi* – name of a tree and its fruit *(Spondias dulcis)*.

Samoan attitude to the distribution of food and other village-produced commodities. The outer villages are beginning to view Apia not as another village but as a commercial market where village-produced foods and other commodities can be sold in much the same way as copra, cacao, and bananas were sold to the trade stores.

There has been a small market in Apia for many years where small quantities of cooked and green taro, *ta'amu*, breadfruit, bananas, and fresh and cooked fish have been sold. But in recent years this has grown into a very considerable market with many sellers and large quantities of Samoan staple foods, fruit, and vegetables, and many non-food commodities which are produced and in common use in the villages. The sellers have not been encouraged or helped in any way by the government or the commercial establishment. The development has been spontaneous.

The study I made of Apia market in 1966 was of a market influenced by unusual circumstances. On Saturday 29 January Western Samoa was hit by a hurricane which caused considerable damage to most of the cash and food crops. Banana, breadfruit, cacao, fruit, and European vegetable crops were destroyed overnight in all parts of Upolu and in most parts of Savai'i. Coconut plantations were damaged, mainly through the loss of immature nuts. Before the hurricane all these commodities had been sold in the Apia market; bananas, copra, and cacao were the country's principal exports, and an overseas market had been developing for taro and several minor crops. In most villages the hurricane caused a fall in cash income from agricultural products and a shortage of staple foodstuffs. The government placed a ban on the export of taro and other staple foods, preferring to retain as much food as possible in the country. The Apia market was thus affected during most of 1966 by unusual supply and demand conditions. This can be illustrated with a comparison between prices ruling in January and July 1966 before and after the hurricane. In July prices were up between 80 and 100 per cent for taro, 100 per cent for tomatoes, about 50 per cent for string beans, and from 100 to 140 per cent for the few, mainly immature, bananas available. Supplies and prices for some vegetables such as cucumbers, chokos, watercress, and cabbage were back to pre-hurricane levels. Prices for some non-food items and for green coconuts were below pre-hurricane levels as villagers attempted to sell more of the commodities readily available in order to buy food.

A survey of the market was carried out on Saturday 30 July, six months after the hurricane. Saturday was always the busiest day in the market, with between two hundred and three hundred sellers turning up, compared with between thirty and fifty during the week days. The survey was limited to a Saturday morning when ten officers of the Department of Agriculture volunteered their time to act as recorders.

The objects of the survey were to find firstly, the variety and quantity of produce offered for sale; secondly, the villages from which the sellers came; and thirdly, the pricing mechanism. With ten volunteer recorders available it was decided to attempt to contact all sellers. The recording work started at 7 a.m. when most sellers were in their places and were prepared for business, and it continued until all sellers had been contacted (between 9 and 9.30 a.m.). At the same time two assistants moved through the market weighing at random selling-units[2] of the more important commodities. I remained in the market all day as an observer. The following information was recorded for each seller: name and sex; village; the type of transport used (bus, lorry, or other) to get to Apia; a list of all commodities offered for sale; the selling-unit and number of selling-units offered for sale for each commodity; and the price asked for each selling-unit.

Several shortcomings of the Apia survey should be mentioned. While an attempt was made to contact all sellers, the haphazard arrangement of the sellers and the possibility of latecomers made it unlikely that this objective was completely attained. Selling continued during the survey and the assistants were instructed to record only produce that they could see and count. This made it certain that some produce would be missed, but the method was considered preferable to one which might delay the recorders for the sake of some doubtful data about what had already been sold. The third drawback concerns the price data which were collected early in the market-day. My observation of the market during the remainder of the day indicated that the price situation continued very much as it had been between 7 and 9.30 a.m. except for a general reduction in prices after about 4 p.m. when the few remaining sellers attempted to sell out. Detailed statistical evidence was not available, however, after about 9.30 in the morning.

The market

On the day of the market survey there were at least 254 sellers (the number contacted). Most sellers had come into Apia by bus, a few by lorry, several on foot, and one by taxi, between 6 and 7 a.m., and each had selected one of four separate locations in the business section of Apia in which to spread out his or her produce. The locations of the market sections are shown in Map 7. They were as follows:

1. The bus-depot. This was the old market mentioned earlier. It had a number of stalls under cover and an area of open ground where produce was displayed. It was privately owned and sellers were charged

[2]In the Apia market nothing is sold by weight. Depending on the type of produce, it will be displayed and offered for sale by the heap, basket or bag-full, bunch or single item. In this chapter I shall include all these forms under the general term 'selling unit'.

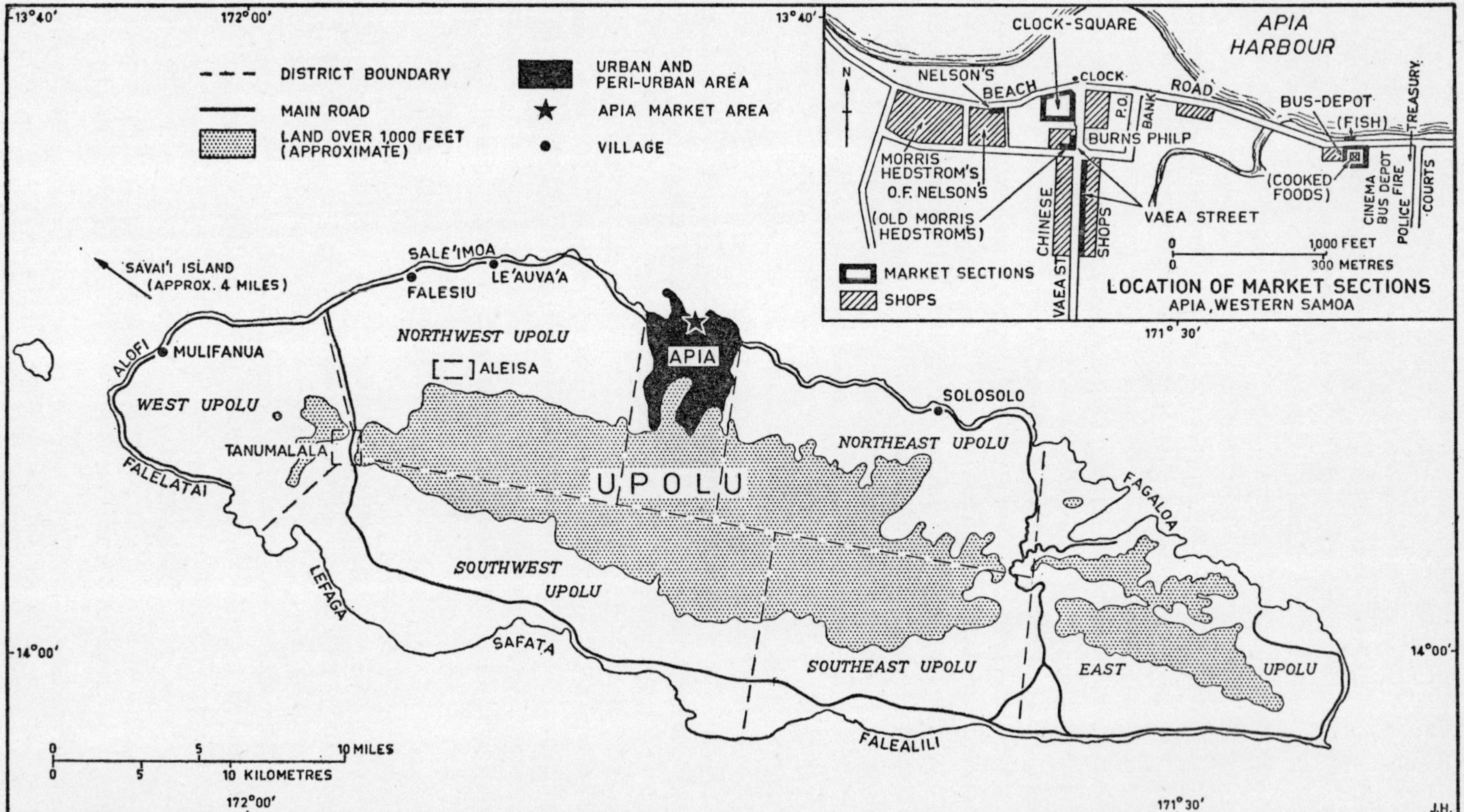

Map 7 *Upolu Island, Western Samoa, showing Districts employed in the text, and roads (inset shows central Apia and the distribution of market-place sites)*

a fee, usually four shillings, for the privilege of selling in this location. Because it adjoined the Apia bus and taxi terminal, was directly in front of the Apia cinema, and was close to a number of medium-sized stores, the law courts, the Police Department, and a number of other government offices, it was located in a very busy part of the town. It contained two specialised sub-sections not found elsewhere in the market – cooked Samoan foods were dispensed from the rear of the open shed, and fishermen sold their catches from the shade of several trees over the road against the beach. For the rest, the bus-depot was a general market with a fairly full range of produce.

2. The clock-square. About one-third of a mile west along Beach Road, at its intersection with Vaea Street, the main road out of Apia to the west, sellers spread out their produce in the sun, or rain, on a vacant building block. This end of town contained the three largest stores, the Bank, the Post Office, and some more government offices and smaller stores. This was quite a general market section and contained most of the non-food commodities supplied in the market.

3. Vaea Street. Half a block from the clock-square, under the veranda of an old Morris Hedstrom store, there was a concentration of vegetable and fruit sellers. Across Vaea Street in front of several Chinese stores there was a concentration of taro sellers.

4. Nelson's. A block further west along Beach Road from the clock-square there was another group of fruit and vegetable sellers on the steps and footpath in front of the O.F. Nelson store.

In addition to these sites in Apia, the road along the north coast to the west of Apia was dotted with many small stalls with the occasional pineapple, bundle of fish, bottle of *sea*, and heap of fruit. There were also two small concentrations of sellers some five and eight miles from Apia. They were not covered successfully in the survey and will not be considered in what follows.

The number of sellers contacted, the value[3] of their produce, and their distribution between the four market sections are summarised in Table V. 1. Details of the commodities offered for sale and their values in each market section will be found in Table V. 2.

The produce

Table V. 1 shows that the total value of all commodities recorded was £754.[4] Of this total, 79 per cent consisted of Samoan foodstuffs, of

[3]Value is calculated on the basis of the selling price per selling-unit of produce and the number of selling-units offered for sale.

[4]The currency in use in 1966 was the Samoan pound, at par with the New Zealand pound and sterling before devaluation in 1967. Conversion to $A would give a false impression of pricing – one shilling would become 12.5 cents – so original currencies are retained in this chapter.

Table V. 1 Number of vendors in each section of Apia market on 30 July 1966, and total value of produce recorded in Samoan pounds (one Samoan pound = $A2.50)

Market section	Number of sellers	Total value of produce (£)
Bus-depot	92	237
Clock-square	83	127
Vaea Street	53	369
Nelson's	26	21
Total market	254	754

Table V. 2 Value in Samoan shillings of each commodity supplied in Apia market on 30 July 1966, distinguishing the separate sections of the market (one Samoan shilling = 12·5 Australian cents)

Commodity	Bus-depot (shillings)	Clock-square (shillings)	Vaea Street (shillings)	Nelson's (shillings)	Total (shillings)
Samoan staples					
taro	3,878	241	5,308	22	9,449
ta'amu	82	298	5	15	400
bananas		288	400		688
breadfruit			48		48
mature coconuts	146	382	122		650
immature coconuts	21	66	111	17	215
lu'au	79	249	113	4	445
banana leaves	10	77	16		103
Total	4,216	1,601	6,123	58	11,998
	(35·1%)	(13·3%)	(51·0%)	(0·6%)	(100%)
Fruit and vegetables					
pawpaw	2	4	12	18	36
pineapple		9		6	15
lemon, lime	1	28	14	5	48
sugar cane			13		13
beans	3	113	118	133	367
cucumber	52	59	162	26	299
tomatoes	2	71	32	147	252
eggfruit	3				3
choko	6	9	3	21	39
pumpkin	3	3	75		81
marrow		10	37	1	48
cabbage	24	7	358	16	405
watercress		5	140		145
radish				2	2
watermelon	2		3		5
ginger	1				1
red peppers				1	1
cocoa beans	5		12	4	21
crushed cocoa			8	3	11
Total	104	318	987	383	1,792
	(5·8%)	(17·7%)	(55·1%)	(21·4%)	(100%)

(continued on next page)

Table V. 2 *(continued)*

Commodity	Bus-depot (shillings)	Clock-square (shillings)	Vaea Street (shillings)	Nelson's (shillings)	Total (shillings)
Seafoods					
fish	27				27
octopus	12				12
limu	25				25
crabs	6				6
Total	70				70
	(100%)				(100%)
Samoan non-food items					
Samoan oil		44		17	61
Samoan tobacco		84			84
'ula	15	139	3		157
'ava		10		10	20
tauaga	79	254	11		344
charcoal		115	22		137
firewood		8			8
laufala (puono)	50				50
pola (blinds)		30			30
salu		11			11
Total	144	695	36	27	892
	(16·2%)	(77·9%)	(4·0%)	(1·9%)	(100%)
Planting material					
taro tops	20		152	5	177
ta'amu				12	12
Total	20		152	17	189
	(10·6%)		(80·4%)	(9·0%)	(100%)
Cooked food	173		20		193
	(89·6%)		(10·4%)		(100%)
Totals	4,727	2,614	7,318	475	15,134
	(31·2%)	(17·3%)	(48·4%)	(3·1%)	(100%)

which taro was by far the most important item (79 per cent of the whole), 12 per cent consisted of introduced vegetables, of which Chinese cabbage, beans, cucumbers, tomatoes, and watercress were the most important, fish and other seafoods contributed less than one per cent, and the remaining 8 per cent was made up with a variety of non-food commodities of which *tauaga*, *'ula*, and charcoal were the largest items.

The relative importance of each section of the market in the total picture, both in value of produce and in types of produce offered for sale, is shown in Table V. 2.

The sellers

Sellers came to the market from most Districts in Upolu Island and a few came from Savai'i Island. Table V. 3 shows the origin of the sellers by District and their location in the Apia market itself. The

Table V. 3 Number of vendors and value of produce in Apia market brought from each District, selling in each market section on 30 July 1966 (one Samoan pound = $A2.50)

District of origin	Bus-depot No. of sellers	Bus-depot Value (£)	Clock-square No. of sellers	Clock-square Value (£)	Vaea Street No. of sellers	Vaea Street Value (£)	Nelson's No. of sellers	Nelson's Value (£)	Total No. of sellers	Total value (£)
Tanumalala & Aleisa	2	(7s)	6	5	12	255			20	260
Northwest	23	20	24	21	26	61	25	21	98	123
Northeast	9	6	45	62					54	68
Southwest	38	175	3	2	14	50			55	227
Southeast	3	13							3	13
West	8	14	3	11	1	3	1	(3s6d)	13	28
Apia	9	9							9	9
Savai'i			2	26					2	26
Total	92	237	83	127	53	369	26	21	254	754

Districts and villages mentioned will be found in Map 7. Table V. 4 summarises the variety and value of commodities by District of origin.

Of the total value of all commodities supplied in the market on the survey day, 35 per cent came with 11 sellers from Tanumalala (total value £205) and 7 sellers from Aleisa (£55). Tanumalala and Alesia, 19 and 9 miles respectively from Apia, are not Samoan villages but areas where the government has leased blocks of agricultural land to part-Samoans. Sixteen of the 28 Tanumalala blocks were leased by Chinese-Samoans, and it was these growers who supplied most of the taro sold in front of the row of Chinese shops in Vaea Street. The 11 Tanumalala sellers and one Aleisa seller, with, altogether, taro worth £215 and other produce worth £40, sold from Vaea Street. They supplied about 80 per cent of the taro sold from this market section and 46 per cent of the taro sold from the market as a whole. Of the remaining 6 sellers from Aleisa, 5 with produce worth £5 between them sold in the clock-square, and 2 with produce worth only 7s between them were at Nelson's.

The three south coast Districts – Lefaga, Safata, and Falealili – sent in altogether 39 per cent of the total value of all produce, including 46 per cent of all taro and 23 per cent of all *lu'au*. This amounted to about £240. There were 29 sellers from Lefaga (£132), 26 from Safata (£96), and 3 from Falealili (£13). Most sold from the bus-depot (41 of the 58 sellers), where they supplied produce worth about £188. Of the rest, 3 (£2) were at the clock-square, and 14 (£50) were in Vaea Street.

Tanumalala, Aleisa, Lefaga, Safata, and Falealili altogether supplied 92 per cent of the taro in the market – about 5·8 tons. With the exception of Falealili District, these areas had been producing taro before the hurricane for the export market. After the hurricane taro exports were banned and the Apia market was the only cash outlet for this production, surplus to the village consumption needs. Growers at Tanumalala and Aleisa had been important suppliers in the Apia market for many years but they also were forced to sell taro in Apia which had been intended for export. It is certain that much of the taro sold in the Apia market before the hurricane came not from Samoan growers in the villages but from the part-Samoan commercial growers from Tanumalala and Aleisa, who also supplied taro under contract to the hospital and other government institutions and schools.

All of the sellers from Tanumalala and 22 from Safata and Lefaga brought their produce to market in locally owned lorries and many paid fares and freight to the lorry owners. Bus fares from the south coast ranged from three to four shillings and freight was usually charged for any large parcels of produce such as a bag of taro or copra. The fares and freight paid on the survey day averaged 7s 6d per seller (including the return fare) and in addition the 43 sellers who paid fees to sell at the bus-depot section were charged an average of 3s 6d per seller. The average cash cost of marketing overall was 9s 5d per seller, which was about 8 per cent of the value of the produce brought in.

Northwest Upolu sent in 16 per cent of the total value of produce – worth about £123. This included 58 per cent of all fruit and vegetables and 50 per cent of all coconuts. Of the 98 sellers from this region, 23, with a total produce worth £20, sold from the bus-depot; 24 (£21) sold from the clock-square; 25 (£21) sold from Nelson's, and 26 (£61) were in Vaea Street in front of the old Morris Hedstrom store.

Northwest Upolu differs from all other regions of Samoa in a number of ways. The area supports the highest density of population outside Apia itself; the villages are so close together along large stretches of the coast that it is impossible to see where one stops and another begins. It is the plantation belt of Samoa, and the existence of large commercial plantations has left many villages with little land. The Samoan lands of northwest Upolu supply very little of the main exports of Samoa and wage employment has become an important source of money income. Many families have moved from the coastal villages, and to some extent from the day-to-day supervision of their family chiefs, and have set up house on inland blocks of agricultural land. They continue to grow taro and other food crops to supply their own and their chief's needs, but an increasing number of them have in addition taken to interplanting European vegetables, mainly string beans, cucumbers, and tomatoes, with the taro. The vegetables are grown as a cash crop for which the Apia market is the only outlet. This embryonic market garden situation is most highly developed in the villages along a five-mile stretch of coast from Le'auva'a to Falesiu,

Table V. 4 Value in Samoan shillings of each commodity supplied in Apia market on 30 July 1966, distinguishing districts of origin of the produce (one Samoan shilling = 12.5 Australian cents)

Commodity	Tanumalala & Aleisa (shillings)	N.W. Upolu (shillings)	N.E. Upolu (shillings)	S.W. Upolu (shillings)	S.E. Upolu (shillings)	W. Upolu (shillings)	Apia (shillings)	Savai'i (shillings)	W. Samoan total (shillings)
Samoan staples									
taro	4,318	463	4	4,118	264	282			9,449
ta'amu		25		52		35		288	400
bananas	400	32				16		240	688
breadfruit	48								48
mature coconuts		256	390			4			650
immature coconuts		186	23			6			215
lu'au	11	26	264	105			39		445
banana leaves		16	77				10		103
Total	4,777	1,004	758	4,275	264	343	49	528	11,998
	39·8%	8·4%	6·3%	35·6%	2·2%	2·9%	0·4%	4·4%	100%
Fruit and vegetables									
pawpaw		32	4						36
pineapple		8	7						15
lemon, lime		21	27						48
sugar cane		13							13
beans	39	296	31	1					367
cucumber	3	288	8						299
tomatoes	26	206	20						252
eggfruit			3						3
choko	6	24		3			6		39
pumpkin	20	38	3	20					81
marrow	4	29		15					48
cabbage	200	43		100		62			405
watercress	50		5	90					145
radish		2							2
watermelon		3	2						5
ginger		1							1
red peppers		1							1
cocoa beans		21							21
crushed cocoa		11							11
Total	348	1,037	110	229		62	6		1,792
	19·4%	57·9%	6·1%	12·8%		3·5%	0·3%		100%

Seafoods									
fish		27							27
octopus		12							12
limu		25							25
crabs		6							6
Total		70							70
		100%							100%
Samoan non-food items									
Samoan oil		23	26			12			61
Samoan tobacco		62		20		2			84
'ula		98				59			157
'ava			10						10
tauaga	9	12	277				46		344
charcoal		22	115						137
firewood			8						8
laufala (puono)		36				14			50
pola			30						30
salu	2		9						11
Total	11	253	475	20		87	46		892
	1·1%	28·4%	53·3%	2·2%		9·8%	5·2%		100%
Planting material									
taro tops	152	5	20						177
ta'amu		12							12
Total	152	17	20						189
	80·4%	9·0%	10·6%						100%
Cooked foods		83	17	20		73			193
		43·0%	8·8%	10·4%		37·8%			100%
Totals	5,288	2,464	1,360	4,564	264	565	101	528	15,134
	35·0%	16·3%	9·0%	30·1%	1·7%	3·7%	0·7%	3·5%	100%

between ten and fifteen miles from Apia. It was from these villages that all but a handful of the northwest Upolu sellers came.

Northeast Upolu was the source of 9 per cent of the value of all produce – amounting to about £68. From this area came 53 per cent of all non-food commodities, 48 per cent of all coconuts, and 62 per cent of all banana and taro leaves. Of the 54 sellers, 45 with a total produce worth £62 sold in the clock-square, and 9 sellers (£6) sold in the bus-depot. Thirty-six of these sellers came from a single village – Solosolo – about fourteen miles from Apia.

The sellers from the north coast all lived within range of a shilling or sixpenny bus fare to market. Few of them carried a large enough quantity of produce to be required to pay a freight charge. The average fare and freight charge to and from Apia was 1s 8d per seller. The 41 sellers who went to the bus-depot were charged an average fee of 2s 3d, which gave an average total cash cost of marketing of about 2s per person or 8 per cent of the value of produce brought in.

Only 13 sellers came from the two areas of Alofi and Falelatai (west Upolu) and they brought in produce valued at only £28. Eight sellers with a total produce worth £14 were at the bus-depot, three (£11) were in the clock-square, one (£3) was in Vaea Street, and one (3s 6d) was at Nelson's. Only two sellers came from Savai'i Island. They brought bananas and *ta'amu* worth £26 and sold them in the clock-square. It had cost them a total of £6 17s in fares and freight (including the return fares), which took over 25 per cent of their possible earnings in the market. It is likely that these two persons had come to Apia for other reasons and had brought along the bananas and *ta'amu* partly to cover their expenses. There were no regular sellers from Savai'i. Nine sellers came from Apia itself and they took produce worth a total of £9 to the bus-depot.

Men and women were present in the market as sellers in almost equal numbers – 142 men and 112 women – but this equality did not extend to the Districts from which they came. Sixty-five of the 80 sellers from Tanumalala, the south coast, and Savai'i were men, and they, of course, brought in not only the heaviest produce but also the most valuable in total. Fifty men and 48 women made up the contingent of vegetable and fruit sellers from the northwest coast but 38 of the 54 sellers of coconuts, taro and banana leaves, fruit and vegetables, and household goods from the northeast coast were women.

Of the 254 sellers in the market 225 (89 per cent) were village Samoans. Collectively they brought in produce valued at £485 (64 per cent of the value of all produce) and earned an average of £2 4s per seller on the day, assuming that they sold all that they brought in at the prices asked early in the day. The 20 part-Samoan sellers from Tanumalala and Aleisa played much larger individual roles by bringing in an average of £13 of produce each. The village Samoans' contribution to the market is significant when seen against a background of village life where there is very little buying and selling of the common commodities sold in the market. Most of the buyers were also Samoans and a fair number were village rather than Apia Samoans. I know from other work done in one of the northwest coast vegetable-producing villages that even before the hurricane many families living on the north coast regularly bought staple foods in the Apia market. The hurricane accentuated the food shortage of the north coast but it was already a permanent feature to a much smaller degree in many north coast villages.

Pricing

In a haphazard market of this kind with no single location, no market authority, and many irregular sellers it could be expected that much of the produce would be sold without the use of scales. In fact no seller used scales and nothing was sold by weight. A system evolved in which most produce was sold in units – heaps, bundles, bags, etc. – which had certain fairly standard prices. Most taro, for example, was displayed and sold by heaps worth 4s, most beans by bundles worth 6d or 1s, most tomatoes by bags worth 1s or 2s, and most fruit by heaps worth 1s. A buyer had no need to ask the price of the great bulk of the produce in the market because it had not varied for years. He had to exercise his powers of observation and compare the selling units of the various sellers for quantity and quality. Price changes were made by changing the size of the heap or bundle, and only rarely by changing the monetary unit. Most produce was sold in units of 1s or multiples of 1s. A few commodities were sold in sixpenny units but none at, say, 1s 6d, or 3d. It was a simple but effective system and it worked well for both sellers and buyers alike.

The regular sellers in the market were skilled in setting out their produce in units which reflected the supply and demand situation on the day. They were able to measure this to some extent by simply looking around the section of the market where they had settled, but once selling started they soon got the feel of the situation. If their units were selling quickly they had a fair idea that the units were bigger than those of their competitors. If they experienced slow sales they knew that the reverse was true. It was a simple matter to rearrange the selling units to make them either larger or smaller as the situation warranted. I have seen such price changes made during the day, particularly towards the end of the day when the few remaining sellers attempted to unload any produce they had left on their hands. The price (size of selling units) also depended to some extent on how long a seller was prepared to wait it out in order to sell his produce. I watched one seller in Vaea Street unload all of his taro between 7 and 7.30 a.m. at a price below that of his competitors; I was told that he did this each Saturday and had built up a number of regular customers. I saw another seller keep his taro bagged until late in the morning, when he set out his heaps priced at 4s, in expectation of higher prices when the shops closed at noon. Seasonal price changes for commodities such as fruit and some vegetables operated in much the same way – by retaining the usual selling unit but increasing or decreasing the quantity. After the hurricane prices for most food commodities rose rapidly but again the standard selling units were retained. I knew some vegetable sellers who were embarassed by the jump in tomato prices after the hurricane. They sold their tomatoes in small brown paper bags at 2s per bag before the hurricane, but after the hurricane they were getting 2s for a quarter the former quantity, and the bags had therefore become much too large. They solved this problem and their embarrassment with a pair of scissors.

There were many irregular sellers in the market and in general it was found that their prices varied more than those of the regulars and that they more frequently sold in larger lots; for example taro by the basket ranging from 8s to 15s rather than by heaps at 4s. Many of these sellers had quite specific reasons for entering the market. The market was not the chief or only source of cash for any of them. Their presence may have been motivated by a special money need within their families or in their villages; perhaps to make the monthly cash gift to the pastor, to meet some village cash subscription, to raise money for a fare to New Zealand, or for any number of possible reasons. These sellers were more likely to see the basket of produce brought into Apia in terms of a quite specific cash need, and their prices could well reflect this rather than the existing market conditions. This type of motivation coupled with only limited and occasional experiences of market conditions explains why their prices varied rather more than those of the regular sellers. Of course they were not fools, and their prices were never far out of line.

Price variations also resulted from the scattered arrangement of sellers between different locations in the business section of Apia. Prices at the bus-depot were generally some 10 per cent higher than in the clock-square, which was one-third of a mile away. Sellers in each section knew little of what was going on in the others and, generally speaking, the buyers tended to go to one or the other rather than to both sections. On the other hand, sellers in the clock-square and Vaea Street maintained fairly similar prices, as buyers moved easily from one to the other. There was a marked price difference between the two groups of vegetable and fruit sellers. Both groups were composed predominantly of regulars but the smaller group in front of Nelson's store in Beach Road was able to tap a steady stream of European shoppers as they passed between the three largest general stores in Apia – Burns Philp's, Morris Hedstrom's, and Nelson's itself – and their prices were always higher than the group in Vaea Street who were a little out of the way for this casual group of impulse buyers. The Vaea Street sellers were known to many Europeans to be cheaper and the more price-conscious went to this section of the market, at least for regular supplies. The volume of produce sold in Vaea Street was more than double that sold in front of Nelson's.

Bargains could be found by buyers willing to look over the market or by those who knew the market well. For example, heaps of taro at 4s were found to vary in weight from 5 to 8 pounds at the bus-depot, and from 5 to 7 pounds in the clock-square. In Vaea Street, most of the heaps were a uniform weight of between 6 and 7 pounds. Bundles of string beans at 1s varied from $1\frac{1}{2}$ to $2\frac{1}{4}$ pounds in the clock-square and from 1 to $1\frac{3}{4}$ pounds at Nelson's. But again in Vaea Street, the sellers outside the old Morris Hedstrom store sold at a steady one-pound bundle for 6d.

Conclusions

It must be remembered that when the survey was made the market was still strongly influenced by the unusual supply and demand conditions which followed the hurricane six months before. But the character of the market was not greatly changed and this allows some general conclusions to be drawn. While quantitatively the market was not normal it is clear that it played an important role in the supply of Samoan foodstuffs to the food-short urban area of Apia and the densely populated villages on the north coast of Upolu. All the food commodities recorded in the survey and a number of others also were regularly sold in the market before the hurricane, and buyers came not only from Apia but also from certain north coast villages. The demand existed, the established commercial firms and the customary mechanism for the distribution of village-produced food failed to satisfy the demand, and the market grew.

The initiative undoubtedly came from part-Samoan growers who were less involved in the Samoan custom and social system and therefore needed to become established in the commercial sector of the economy. They were joined by Samoans from certain north coast villages, in which it is fair to say the custom and social system had been eroded by many decades of involvement in the commercial sector and close contact with Apia itself. So the survey found the part-Samoan group of sellers numerically small, but its contribution to the market supply quantitatively large. The north coast villages sent in a large number of sellers, many of whom had become regular participants in the market, but quantitatively their contribution was small.

It should be said that the market was a serious affair and most of the sellers were concerned to earn a cash income in it. For many sellers it was their only source of money. Few sellers regarded it primarily as a social outing, although for some irregular sellers from outer villages it undoubtedly had this aspect. The seriousness of the market and its commercial sophistication is demonstrated by its pricing system, which was extremely sensitive to changes in supply and demand conditions.

VI

Melanesian Mélange: The Market at Vila, New Hebrides

H. C. Brookfield, Paula Brown Glick, and Doreen Hart

The study of Vila market formed part of a multi-purpose research project undertaken in the capital town of the New Hebrides Condominium in 1965. The market provides one of the most regular and readily observable points of contact between town and country and between the various peoples of the area. It has much of interest from both these viewpoints, for rural communities do not participate equally in the market and the pattern of trading illustrates many aspects of Vila's multiplex economic and cultural life. The market of Vila is small and has a minor place in the distributive system of the community. Yet its produce is quite varied, and both buyers and sellers are of diverse ethnic origin. It serves the inhabitants of Vila and the surrounding region with a place where fresh produce, and a few other products, may be bought and sold, money may be earned, and the social interchange of the market-place is pursued.

Field work was carried out by H. C. Brookfield and Paula Brown Glick, with a number of local assistants among whom particular mention should be made of Miss Teresa Franklin and Mrs Caroline Leaney. Mrs Hart carried out most of the later analysis in Canberra and participated in the writing of the paper. Mrs Amy Singh of Canberra and Miss Suzi Matoba of New York also worked on the data.

We are indebted to the Australian National University for its generous support of this research, to the British Residency and the Résidence de France in Vila for their co-operation and aid in securing local assistants, and to the people of Vila and Efaté for their tolerance of our inquisitiveness. Vila has changed greatly since this survey, but the present tense means 1965 throughout.

Until late in the nineteenth century, the town and peri-urban area of Vila were the locale of the garden land of a Melanesian community whose residences were mostly concentrated on Fila Island, in the bay. Vila's harbour, administrative, and commercial activities have made it a political, social, economic, educational, religious, and commercial centre for French and British interests in the New Hebrides. It soon developed into a typical colonial town, focused upon its harbour, the entry point of goods and people, and the export point of its products – chiefly copra, with a few other tree and animal products. It also became the administrative centre of the New Hebrides' complex British, French, and Condominium governments, missions, and commerce. The two largest firms conduct, within the island group, the business of buying export crops and distributing imported and manufactured products. Both of these are branches of large firms centred in New Caledonia and Australia respectively. Many other businesses are branches of French-New Caledonian organisations.

Since 1900, with the growth of government and commerce, many people have come to Vila to take part in these activities. Plantations were established throughout the southwestern lowland of Efaté, and the town has grown at their expense. French, British, and other European nationalities were represented in the administrative, professional, managerial, clerical, sales, and technical occupations. Soon the population included Asians as well: Chinese and Japanese shopkeepers selling mostly to New Hebridean natives, and Vietnamese who came on work contracts for the plantations in the 1920s, later became a middle class of technicians and small entrepreneurs in town and country. Still later, as most of the Vietnamese were repatriated, there was an influx of Pacific islanders from Tahiti, Wallis, Futuna, New Caledonia, Fiji, and Tonga with some education and skills. New Hebridean natives have come to Vila from all the islands in the group, mostly to work as unskilled or semi-skilled labourers.

The town population is as varied as any that might be found in an urban community. Yet the close-built area of urban Vila has a population of fewer than 3,000. At a census taken as part of our project in June 1965, 2,646 persons were enumerated in the town and in institutions, such as the prisons and schools, located within it. In the whole area of the lowland of southwestern Efaté is a non-village population of 4,624, of whom 487 are on plantations or in schools located in the rural area, 1,491 in the peri-urban areas around the town, and the balance in the town itself. Of these people 2,786 are New Hebrideans from all over the group, 745 are Europeans, 476 Métis and others, 304 Asians, and 313 people of other Pacific islands. The dominant colonial power is France via New Caledonia, for most shore-based larger businesses in Vila are subsidiaries of New Caledonian firms.

Despite this French dominance in the cultural life of the town, few New Hebrideans speak French: until very recently most rural schooling was provided by Australian-based missions, and English and Pidgin *(Bêche-la-mar)* are the commonest non-native tongues.

There are few specialty or tourist shops in Vila. But the people of the area get most of their daily necessities in Vila, and may choose from a number of general stores handling foodstuffs, hard and soft goods. While communication in both French and English is possible in the three largest shops which cater especially to European and Asian tastes, French-speaking customers predominate in two of them, English-speakers in the third. The Chinese, who usually speak English and Pidgin, and the Vietnamese, speaking French and Pidgin, sell mainly to New Hebridean townspeople and villagers on a trip to town. The resulting segregation of commercial activity is only partial; shortages of goods and special needs often break customers' habits.

Vila has grown quickly in recent years: a core of older housing remains in the northern part of the town, but around it are extensive low-density suburbs. The commercial axis of the town is the Rue Higginson, running along the waterfront and named after a London-Irishman who sought to make the New Hebrides a colony of France. Here are a complex of Chinese and Vietnamese shops at the northern end, some modern European shops and offices, and the large but unsightly buildings of the two main company stores, one New Caledonian (Comptoirs Françaises des Nouvelles-Hébrides, generally known by the name of its parent Nouméa company, Ballande) and one Australian (Burns Philp). Between these two, on a narrow strip of open land between the road and the harbour, is the site of the weekly market. Each Friday up to a hundred sellers gather here to offer foodstuffs for sale. They include mainly women from villages in southwestern and north Efaté, and a few New Hebridean, Chinese, Métis, Vietnamese, and European men. Buyers are similarly diverse. The market does not supply all the vegetable needs of the town. Many New Hebrideans, especially in the peri-urban area, have small gardens of their own, for their shanties are not closely built. Some natives from the villages of Efaté go home at week-ends and bring fresh foods to town. Europeans in particular buy imported Australian produce from the shops. Some hawkers tour the suburbs, and during the week smaller groups of sellers offer produce on the steps of Ballande store and elsewhere along the Rue Higginson.

With the aid of assistants we surveyed Vila market on each of four Fridays in July 1965,[1] recording for each seller the quantities of

[1]This period was determined by the availability of our New Hebridean assistants, who were students of Kawenu Teachers' Training College, employed by us during their vacation. The main employment of these students was on a

various goods brought to market, the prices asked where possible, and some supplementary information. Later in the survey, our assistants observed the sellers in their sector of the market and recorded as many transactions as they could for each seller. Unfortunately, only the first Friday was wholly fine; the third and fourth were wet. Since the market is in the open, it is greatly affected by the weather.

We also carried out some associated field work among the growers of market produce. It is difficult to say how representative of the whole year was the period of our inquiry. Data obtained from a number of growers suggests that many of the vegetables, some native staples, and even some fruit, are available at all times of the year. Yams are seasonal, harvested between April and July, and cabbage, tomatoes, onions, and some other European vegetables are also in peak supply during these months. Some tropical fruits were out of season or in poor supply in July. During the period of our survey, there was a marked falling off in the supply of native staples, especially yams, and some increase in the supply of European vegetables. In the central New Hebrides 1965 was a wet year, but severe droughts sometimes occur between May and December, and these would undoubtedly affect the supply of produce. Probably the market was as well supplied during our survey as at any period of the year.

The structure and organisation of the market

We divide the sellers into two categories, village women and specialists. The village women come into the market from four of the six villages of southwestern Efaté – Erakor, Pango, Fila Island, and Mele – and from three villages in northern Efaté – Leleppa, Mosso, and Siviri (Map 8). For them, selling in the market is an occasional activity, additional to subsistence cultivation, housekeeping, and some other income-producing activities, such as helping in copra production or occasional wage work. Forty-one per cent of males over the age of fifteen in the villages around Vila are in paid employment in town and country, and some of the children attend Vila schools. Little of the food sold by the women in the market is distinguishable from household food. However, many women prepare and sell packages of cooked food *(laplap)*, and some of them sell nothing else; this, then, is production

census of Vila and environs, results of which will be reported elsewhere. The market inquiry had to be fitted in with this program. Co-operation of sellers was good, though by the fourth week we found that some were tiring of our observation. We also questioned buyers on two market-days. Inquiry was carried out mainly in New Hebridean Pidgin *(Bêche-la-mar)* among the sellers, and also in English and French among the buyers. In this account the present tense used to describe market characteristics means 1965, unless the sense denotes otherwise.

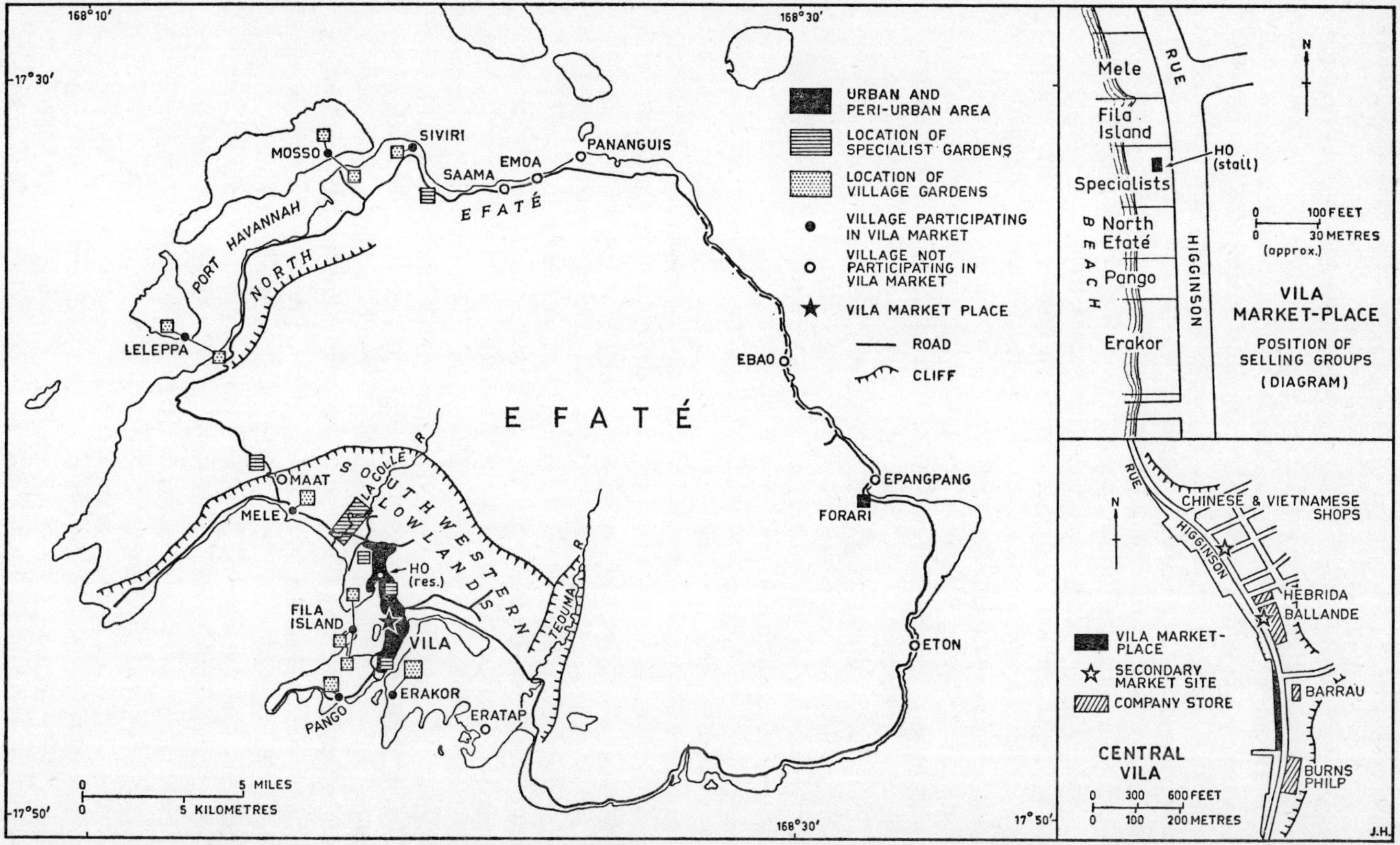

Map 8 *Efaté Island, New Hebrides, showing places supplying Vila market, and roads (insets show central Vila and Vila market-place)*

specifically for the market. The small quantities of shell gathered for sale are also solely for the market.

In our other category are the 'specialists', mostly men, whose main economic activity is growing (occasionally augmented by buying) foods and selling in the market. These we have again subdivided into New Hebrideans and others, including Vietnamese, Chinese, mixed-bloods, and Europeans. Many of them hire workers at $16 to $28 per month. All but two of the specialists live in the southwestern lowland, on land bought or rented at quite varied rates from land owners who are mainly European, or from villagers on reserve land. Some are of local origin, some from other islands. Some have sold in the market for a long time, even sold vegetables to the American forces in Vila and North Efaté during World War II. Others are more recent participants, often using only tiny pockets of rented land for rather unbalanced vegetable production. One Vietnamese, formerly a shopkeeper in north Vila, has entered market gardening only recently because his new shop is not sufficiently profitable. He hawks goods around the northern part of the town in his land-rover, and has only recently started selling in the market, which he finds more profitable. Some specialists are extremely poor, and have to eke out their small market income with other work. Three men stand out. One, mainly New Hebridean, but with Seychellese ancestors of whose French naval forbears he is very proud, cultivates some twenty acres on the plateau behind Mele for a range of tree crops, and has about one and a half acres under a well-balanced range of European vegetables. He produces tree crop products for export sale. The second, a European copra planter in North Efaté, has a small fenced area under market garden crops. He has for some time sold vegetables through the Australian company store in Vila, and entered the market only in July 1965. The third, a Vietnamese, whom we here call Ho, does not grow vegetables himself, but buys from a number of growers at his house, just over a mile north of the town. He also buys in bulk within the market, from village women and other specialists. He alone makes marketing his only occupation.

The market has not always had this composition. Formerly, the supply of vegetables to Vila was largely in the hands of former Vietnamese plantation workers. These Vietnamese were drawn almost entirely from inland Tonkin, and by the end of World War II had all completed their contracts. They were nearly all adherents of the Viet Minh at this time, and after many were repatriated in 1946 and 1947, the French halted all further repatriation for fifteen years. During this period, the Vietnamese concentrated into and around the towns of Santo and Vila where they took up businesses and trades, became the artisan force of the population, and also the market gardeners. Finally nearly 2,000 were repatriated in 1963, including 787 from Vila. The few remaining opted to stay permanently in the New Hebrides, and a large proportion of them were already well integrated with the French population of the group.[2] Around Vila the Vietnamese had settled both north and south of the town, and market gardens were established in these areas. After their houses were vacated in 1963 they were speedily reoccupied by New Hebrideans and other Pacific islanders, but very few of these turned to market gardening. In mid-1965, only two years after the repatriation, a new pattern of supply was not yet firmly established.

Each group of vendors in the market occupies its own specific area, as shown in Map 8 (inset). These locations are relatively fixed, though the boundaries shift according to the number of sellers of each group present on any occasion. The specialists occupy the central position, grouped around a roofed shelter erected for his own use by Ho. Here there is some jostling for position, but on either flank the villagers squat on the ground behind their produce, in a single or double line, backs to the water.

Transport into the market is by varied means, but mainly by taxi. Fila Islanders draw up their canoes on the beach behind the market. There is no form of control or regulation, and sellers are neither licensed nor inspected. Buyers come on foot, or park their cars on a piece of waste ground opposite, and walk along the market.

Vendors do not arrive all at once. First to arrive are some specialists and the women from Mele village, who are often in the market before 8 a.m. and leave early. By 11 a.m. they have been joined by most of the other specialists and women from the North Efaté villages, but there is still little activity. About 11 a.m. the Fila Island women arrive by canoe or launch, and trade in cooked food becomes brisk when the lunch hour begins for town workers. Pango and Erakor women mostly arrive between 1.30 and 2.30 p.m., so that the number of vendors reaches a peak about 2.30 p.m., after which the Fila Islanders who have sold their cooked food, and Mele women who sell produce in quantity, begin to leave. Most others remain through the afternoon. The peak trading period occurs between 4 p.m. and 4.45 p.m., after work in the town ceases for the day. The number of buyers then reaches a peak, though we never counted more than forty-one present at any one time, so that buyers are always outnumbered by vendors. Little business is done after 5 p.m. and the market then empties rapidly.

There are also differences in the way that goods are presented for sale. Many of the village women have baskets or boxes of food which they place in a group, and then retire in a cluster at some distance from

[2]A fuller account of the post-war history and repatriation of the Vietnamese in both the New Hebrides and New Caledonia is given by Doumenge (1966:195-202).

their wares, sometimes leaving the area, so that a potential buyer may have some difficulty in finding the seller. The specialists take some trouble to package and present their goods to buyers, and the European planter's display included a blackboard listing goods and prices.

Table VI. 1 shows the pattern of attendance by vendors during the period of our survey. The effect of weather is noticeable, especially on the third day, when it rained steadily most of the day. The fourth was also mostly rainy. The first Friday was the monthly pay-day. Not surprisingly, the specialists are more regular in their attendance than the villagers, except those of Fila Island. The most irregular were the women of Mosso and Siviri in North Efaté – the remotest participating villages. However, Leleppa women from the same area were present in good numbers on all four dates.

Table VI. 1 Attendance at Vila market on each survey date in July 1965 by vendors of each group, and the contribution of each group to the total supply of produce by value

	Day 1	Day 2	Day 3	Day 4	Total visits	A	B	C	D ($A)	E (%)
Villagers										
Pango	9	14	6	5	34	19	0	1·79	3.84	5·8
Erakor	24	22	19	24	89	50	2	1·78	6.29	24·8
Fila Island	21	26	20	21	88	36	5	2·44	2.93	11·4
Mele	12	7	6	9	34	19	1	1·79	3.56	5·3
North Efaté	15	15	8	13	51	34	2	1·50	8.42	19·0
Specialists										
New Hebridean	8	10	8	10	36	13	5	2·80	10.39	16·5
Other	4	5	5	5	19	7	3	2·80	20.46	17·2

A Total number of individuals ever attending the market during the survey period.
B Persons who attended on all four dates.
C Average times attended by individual sellers.
D *Average value* of goods brought to market per seller per visit.
E Percentage of the *total value* over four weeks ($2,261.73) provided by the sellers of each group.

The produce brought to market

We divided the goods brought to market into seven classes, as follows:

1. Native staple foods: breadfruit, green and dry coconuts, manioc, sugar cane, sweet potatoes, taro *(Colocasia* and *Xanthosoma)*, yams *(Dioscorea alata*, *esculenta*, *bulbifera)*.

2. Other native foods: arrowroot, 'island cabbage', 'millionaire's salad' (the inflorescence of the coconut palm), nuts, snake beans, various leaves and greens.

3. Animal produce: bats, birds, crabs, eggs, fish, fowl, lobsters, pigs, pork, octopus, shellfish, turtles.

4. Cooked food: cake, fish, fowl, *laplap* (a soft cake of grated taro, yam or banana, cooked with coconut cream), plates of soup and rice.

5. Fruit: bananas (several varieties), grapefruit, grenadillas, lemons, limes, oranges, pawpaws, pineapples, soursop, watermelons.

6. Vegetables: aubergines, beans, beetroot, carrots, Chinese cabbage, English cabbage, chokos, corn, cucumbers, kohlrabi, lettuce, green onions, parsley, peas, green peppers, pumpkins, radishes, tomatoes, turnips, watercress.

7. Curios: baskets, combs, flowers, grass skirts, model canoes, necklaces, paddles, shells, spears.

With the exception of a small quantity of manufactured goods and shells, the market is supplied only with foodstuffs. One man also sells cigarettes, but there is no trading in utensils, clothing, or other imported produce. There is little attempt to provide for the potential tourist market. Though an overseas ship with a number of Australian tourists was in port on one market day, there was no increase in the quantity of curios on sale. Shells are sold mainly to a few regular European collectors who live in Vila.

In recording the produce brought into the market by each vendor, our assistants noted also the selling value put on the goods by the vendor. This was not done in every case, so in totalling the data we were left with a minority of produce described in quantity terms alone, and often by such packages as 'boxes', 'bunches', or 'baskets'. Knowledge of the market enabled us to make some estimate of the quantities included in these packages, but to obtain comparable data it was necessary to reduce all goods to value terms. To achieve this Mrs Leaney listed all goods with quantities and prices asked, averaged the prices so obtained, and then applied these average prices to the goods which were listed in quantity terms alone.[3] These computations form the basis of most of our tabulations.

Almost all prices were quoted in Australian shillings and pence, the commonest currency in the New Hebrides in 1965, though French Pacific francs were more important in larger-scale commerce. Australian currency was converted to a decimal basis in 1966, and Australian dollars and cents are now used in the New Hebrides. All values are given here in Australian dollars, which are worth 100 French Pacific francs so that 1 cent is now exactly equivalent to 1 franc.

Table VI. 2 analyses the goods brought into the market by produce classes and days. The dominance of vegetables, native staples, and

[3]The resulting error is probably less than 10 per cent, though, as noted below, there is some variation in prices asked in different parts of the market, which was not taken into account. There was also some difficulty in identifying certain of the goods listed: 'strong' turned out finally to be 'citron', but 'wofly' remained unidentifiable to the last. In all this work Mrs Leaney's intimate knowledge of the market and of the produce was invaluable.

Table VI. 2 Percentage of the total value of produce offered in Vila market on four days in July 1965 within each produce class

Produce class	Day 1 (%)	Day 2 (%)	Day 3 (%)	Day 4 (%)	All four days (%)	All four days ($)
Native staple foods	30·2	29·3	21·2	22·9	26·8	605.53
Other native foods	1·0	0·7	1·4	1·5	1·0	24.15
Animal produce	10·3	8·2	7·4	8·0	8·7	196.20
Cooked food	12·3	18·0	15·0	14·2	14·9	336.00
Fruit	20·3	20·0	22·2	15·4	19·4	439.49
Vegetables	24·2	21·4	32·2	35·2	27·2	615.96
Curios	1·7	2·4	0·6	2·8	2·0	44.40
Total %	100·0	100·0	100·0	100·0	100·0	
Total value	$711.53	$667.31	$368.52	$514.37		$2,261.73

fruit is clear on all dates. However, there was some fluctuation, apart from the fairly large variation in total volume from day to day. The proportion of native staples declined while that of vegetables increased. Yams were certainly in declining supply, and the produce of vegetable gardens was coming increasingly on to the market during July, but it may be that variations in trading results, which we shall discuss below, were also affecting the supply.

In Table VI. 3 goods brought into the market on all four days combined are analysed in terms of their origin. It will be readily apparent that different groups of sellers concentrated on different classes of produce. Thus 61 per cent of the offerings from Erakor village comprised native staples, and this one village provided 57 per cent of all the native staples on sale. The much smaller number of Mele women also offered mostly native staples and fruit, augmenting these with European vegetables, while a large proportion of fish and meats came from Erakor. Seventy per cent of the produce offered by Fila Islanders was cooked food, and this comprised 53 per cent of all cooked food on sale, the balance coming mainly from North Efaté. Sixty-eight per cent of the goods offered by New Hebridean specialists, and 76 per cent of those offered by non-New Hebridean specialists were European vegetables, and these two groups of sellers provided no less than 89 per cent of the total of vegetables offered. Forty-four per cent of the North Efaté produce was fruit, comprising 43 per cent of all the fruit on sale; 47 per cent of the small quantity of manufactured goods on sale came from Pango village.

Participation in the market

The significance of these specialisations becomes apparent in the context of the very uneven participation in the market among the population of western Efaté. In Table VI. 4 we show the population of the

Table VI. 3 Value and percentage of produce offered in Vila market on all survey dates combined, within each produce class and by vendors of each group

Produce class		Erakor	Pango	Fila Island	Mele	N. Efaté	Specialists, New Hebridean	Specialists, other	Total
Native staple foods	$	343.77	38.18	8.75	79.71	63.95	62.57	8.60	605.53
	%	61·4	29·2	3·4	65·8	14·9	16·7	2·2	26·8
Other native foods	$	6.80	2.60	0.60	2.55	1.60	9.20	0.80	24.15
	%	1·2	2·0	0·2	2·1	0·4	2·5	0·2	1·0
Animal produce	$	89.50	9.90	27.25	—	47.75	0.80	21.00	196.20
	%	16·0	7·6	10·6	—	11·1	0·2	5·4	8·7
Cooked food	$	15.70	31.80	179.00	2.40	104.30	2.80	—	336.00
	%	2·8	24·3	69·5	2·0	24·3	0·7	—	14·9
Fruit	$	86.39	10.79	28.95	17.96	188.50	43.95	62.95	439.49
	%	15·4	8·2	11·2	14·8	43·9	11·8	16·2	19·4
Vegetables	$	14.20	16.90	2.80	16.36	16.10	254.10	295.50	615.96
	%	2·5	12·9	1·1	13·5	3·8	67·9	76·0	27·2
Curios	$	3.60	20.70	10.30	2.10	7.00	0.70	—	44.40
	%	0·7	15·8	4·0	1·8	1·6	0·2	—	2·0
Total value	$	559.96	130.87	257.65	121.08	429.20	374.12	388.85	2,261.73
	%	100·0	100·0	100·0	100·0	100·0	100·0	100·0	100·0

island, other than the 2,646 living in urban Vila, and perhaps 1,000 living on plantations, at schools, and in the mining town of Forari on the east coast. We show also the distance of each population centre from Vila market by the most direct route, generally by road, but also by road and canoe. The legal cost of a journey one way by taxi, which is the commonest form of transport overland, is given in the third column. Taxi rates per mile are much cheaper within the southwestern lowland than for journeys outside it: to North Efaté the minimum rate is about 50 per cent higher per mile than nearer Vila, and actual rates,

Table VI. 4 Population of localities in Efaté Island, New Hebrides, with real and economic distance of each locality from Vila market

		Population (P)	Distance miles (D)	Costs* (C) ($)
A	Fila Island	328	0·9	0.22
	Peri-urban N. †	972	1·2	0.40
	Peri-urban S. †	519	1·2	0.30
	Rural, non-village †	487	3·1	0.90
	Erakor	374	2·8	0.67
	Pango	291	3·4	0.90
	Mele	698	5·3	1.30
	Maat	163	6·7	1.62
B	Eratap	170	7·8	1.88
	Leleppa	255	16·2	5.72
	Mosso	150	23·3	8.25
	Siviri	87	24·9	8.80
	Eton	130	26·9	9.46
	Saama	110	28·0	9.90
	Emoa	99	29·2	10.34
	Pananguis	226	31·1	11.00
	Epangpang	12	34·2	12.10
	Ebao	67	39·8	14.08

A Population figures *de facto* from A.N.U. census, July 1965.
B Population figures *de jure* from French recensement, 1963.

*One-way taxi cost according to legal scale where available, elsewhere assessed at modal rate per mile for each part of the island. In the southwestern area the modal rate is 24 cents per mile (range 19-35 cents). In the northern and eastern parts of the island the modal rate to and from Vila is 35 cents (range 29-39 cents). Where a canoe journey is involved this is costed at the prevailing taxi rate. Round-trip rates are between 32 and 45 cents in the southwest (mode about 39 cents), to and from the rest of the island 36 to 48 cents, and with a mode of 42 cents. Since market trips must of necessity be two one-way trips, these latter rates are not applicable.

†Approximately central locations are used for distance and cost values calculated for these areas.

Note: These figures do not include the Compagnie Française des Phosphates d'Océanie mining town at Forari (population of town and environs about 1,000 in 1967), or a number of plantations and schools outside the southwestern lowland.

as we shall see below, are higher yet. The 'economic distance' of North Efaté from Vila is thus greater than the 'real distance'.

Not all villages in southwestern Efaté supply the market. Nothing comes from either Eratap, which has no direct road, or Maat, a recent resettlement from Ambrym Island. Most of the specialists are either in the peri-urban area or else in the rural area to the north. With two exceptions all are within 4 miles of the market. One is 7·8 miles away, and the other, the European planter on the north coast, is 25·4 miles from town. This man uses his own transport, but at an operating cost probably not much less than the legal round-trip taxi fare of $11.20. In view of the high cost it is surprising that villagers from North Efaté, up to 25 miles from the market, should participate at all.

That the extent of the interrelationship between any two centres should theoretically be directly proportional to the product of their populations and inversely proportional to the distance between them follows from *prima-facie* reasoning: it has been demonstrated empirically by Reilly (1929) and especially by Zipf (1949: 369-71 and 386-409). If other things were equal, we might expect participation in the market to vary according to this principle. In Efaté, Vila is the only urban centre and the only market;[4] all places are linked by road to the capital. We calculated interaction values for each place, using both simple distance P/D (population/distance) of each community, population of Vila being constant, and also economic distance P/C (population/cost). The fall-off in expected interaction outside the Vila lowland is rapid, and we would expect only 2 per cent of the whole interaction – here measured as market supply – to come from places outside the southwestern lowland. Maat and Eratap, both of which supply nothing, each have more than twice the expected interaction value of Leleppa. In Table VI. 5 we restrict ourselves to the places actually supplying the market. The P/C values are totalled and percentaged to yield the expected relative contribution of each locality, and this is then compared with the actual percentage of the value of goods brought to market, taking all goods, and also vegetables (which show much closer correspondence). The North Efaté anomaly is outstanding. In this analysis we have notionally attributed the contribution of the specialists to the peri-urban area. The largest selling specialist is the middleman Ho, who buys nearly all his produce from New Hebrideans, both village producers and specialists. We have seen him buy boxes of produce from village women as they arrive at the market, and break up the quantities into small units. However, we do not know what proportion of the food he sells comes from different locales. It is possible that his bulk purchases are taken from villages which are poorly represented in the market.

[4]Forari had no independent system of fresh food supply up to July 1965.

Table VI. 5 Theoretical expectation of the contribution of each supplying locality to Vila market on the basis of population/economic distance compared with the actual percentage contribution from each locality in July 1965

	Contribution expected all four days (P/C) (%)	Total brought all four days (%)	Vegetables brought all four days (%)
Total supply to the market from the participating area			
Fila Island	7·35	11·4	0·5
Peri-urban*	70·35	33·9	89·8
Erakor	8·35	24·8	2·3
Pango	4·84	5·8	2·7
Mele	8·03	5·3	2·7
North Efaté	1·09	19·0	2·6
Supply from the villages only			
Fila Island	24·77	17·19	
Erakor	28·16	37·36	
Pango	16·31	8·73	
Mele	27·08	8·08	
North Efaté	3·67	28·64	

*Peri-urban is here included as the location of most of the specialists, including the numerous small gardeners who sell to Ho.

Note: The expected values are obtained by totalling the P/C values from Table VI. 4, then expressing values for each locality as a percentage, to compare with the percentage actually supplied. Calculations were based on distances measured in kilometres on the 1:50,000 map of Efaté and converted into miles.

Deleting the specialists from consideration, and paying attention only to the villagers, we find that both North Efaté and Erakor supply above expectation, while Pango, and especially Mele, are far below. The curious fact emerges that a strongly disproportionate contribution comes from people who are separated from Vila by a journey which includes an interchange from water to road transport, while a less than proportionate contribution comes from people with a simple journey, either by road or water – quite the reverse of normal experience.

With anomalies of this order, it is not possible to simulate the supply of Vila market by a standard explanatory model. But the anomalous aspects will serve to explain aspects of the trade and viability of the market, as we shall see as we go forward.

The trade of the market

Buyers approach the market and inspect the goods on sale. They are not importuned to buy. Many buyers walk the full length of the market but the majority of all ethnic groups spend longest in the central area, where the specialists are, and some buy only in this section. Except for a few commodities of universally standard price, such as *laplap* which is always 10 cents per portion, the price of an individual item or basket is quoted on application to the seller. Prices asked are usually, and among village sellers almost always, in multiples of 5 cents and 10 cents (i.e. 6d and 1s), but for small items 2·5 cents (3d) was also used. Pricing is rather approximate: thus baskets of oranges normally sell for 50 cents or $1, but rarely for intermediate prices. Dry coconuts are almost always priced at 5 cents each. The widest variation is in the prices of native staple foods. Large yams are sold individually at prices ranging between 20 cents and $2, depending on size and variety. Baskets of small yams, and bunches and baskets of island taro *(Colocasia* sp.*)* and Fiji taro *(Xanthosoma* sp.*)* show similar variation. Village sellers offer most commodities in larger packages than the central, specialist sellers, and the unit prices are thus somewhat lower than those obtained by sellers who break up their goods into smaller lots. These quantities are more suited to non-European buyers and buyers for groups living in clubs and institutions. But the larger institutions obtain foodstuffs from other sources as well as in the market. The sellers in the central area are able to charge higher prices than the average by exploiting the habits of European buyers and selling in smaller quantities. The average prices that we obtained and applied are thus generally a little higher than the mode.[5]

Ho, the Vietnamese middleman, exploits this situation systematically. In addition to buying vegetables and fruit from growers at his own house, he also buys quantities within the market. Sometimes he both buys and sells in bulk packages such as baskets – perhaps buying for 50 cents and selling for $1 but sometimes without profit. Most commonly he buys in bulk and sells in smaller quantities, making a useful

[5]Examples of average prices are:

	$		$
Native staples:		*Fruit: (cont.)*	
large yams, each	1.11	grapefruit, each	0.09
small yams, baskets	1.12	oranges, baskets	0.98
island taro, baskets/bunches	0.73	oranges, each	0.04
Fiji taro, baskets/bunches	0.53	lemons, baskets	1.25
breadfruit, each	0.10	lemons, six	0.16
Meat and fish:		watermelons, each	0.40
fowls, each	2.00	*Vegetables:*	
lobsters, each	0.96	cucumbers, each	0.13
octopus, each	0.65	green onions, bunches	0.12
Fruit:		lettuces, rings	0.13
bananas, bunches	0.59	watercress, bunches	0.15
bananas, hands	0.15	tomatoes, bags	0.35
pawpaws, each	0.15	*Manufactures:*	
pineapples, each	0.23	grass skirts, each	1.25

(Lettuce rings are four to six small soft heads threaded on to a sliver of bamboo bent and tied in a ring.)

profit but one which is difficult for anyone, including himself, to estimate accurately.[6] Ho often varies his prices in a seemingly random manner from one customer to the next. Sometimes he will give away oranges and other fruit to accompany a sale of goods. By his enterprise, he provides the customers with the kind of selling they want, and has by far the largest volume of sales. He also relieves other vendors of much produce of which they might not otherwise dispose. The other specialists, and certainly the villagers, exhibit little of this more refined sales technique. Sometimes well-known and regular customers will be sold goods at prices below ruling levels, but there is little or no bargaining anywhere in the market, nor is there any reduction of prices for goods left unsold towards the end of the day. Unsold goods are taken away from the market, to be given to friends, eaten, wasted, or offered again for sale on a later occasion. We made an attempt to record the amount of produce taken away from the market, but with the open, formless nature of this market, it is often difficult to know when a seller is about to leave; this recording was so patchy that no use could be made of it.

If the function of the market were restricted to its largest component, sale to Europeans, it would be commercially a very imperfect market. A high proportion of vendors present and price their goods badly, or sell to Ho at prices they would not accept from a customer. Many goods are offered for sale only in large packages, thus making them unacceptable to the small European household. Only among the central group of specialists do we find practices adapted to the requirements of the European households. The European planter who entered the market in 1965 hoped to educate the vendors in price policy, but his early efforts left him very disappointed. Doubtless, an improvement would occur if the market were housed, with tables and stands on which the goods of all vendors could be displayed and compared, with licence fees charged against provision of maintenance services. The villagers at present dominate the market numerically, but conduct a small proportion of the total retail market transactions, and these are notably concentrated among non-European buyers. Villagers mainly sell cooked food to town-dwelling islanders, and quantities of staple foods and fruits to large households or distributors; they sell few fresh vegetables in small quantities to any category of buyers.

The pattern of buying

In the third and fourth weeks of our survey, after the basic work was

[6]Examples are: bananas bought by the bunch at 40 cents, sold for 10 cents or 20 cents per hand; oranges bought by the basket for 50 cents or $1, sold at 10 cents for three; green onions bought by the case for $1, sold at 10 cents per bunch; lemons bought at $1.50 for a large bag, sold in small bags at 20 cents per bag.

done and good rapport established between each assistant and his group of vendors, we attempted systematic recording of sales. The object was to note down, for each transaction, the name of vendor, ethnic category of buyer, price and quantity of produce. Substantial, but by no means complete success was achieved, the greatest omissions being among the village sellers, where our assistants were more thinly spread.

The result is set out in Table VI. 6, from which it is clear that the different categories of buyers distribute their trade in very different ways. European buyers deal almost exclusively with the specialists, and go to the villagers only for curios and a little fish and meat.[7] Europeans spent 89 per cent of their recorded purchases on fruit and vegetables, compared with 93 per cent for the 'Others' group and 84 per cent for the Asians, but only 61 per cent for the Fijians and 52 per cent for the New Hebrideans. The 'Others' group consists in about equal numbers of Métis and of Tahitians and Wallisians; their buying pattern is similar to that of the Europeans and Asians. The Fijians, on the other hand, buy substantial quantities of native staple foods from the villagers and the new Hebridean specialists. The major trading partners of the villagers, however, are the New Hebridean buyers.

The specialist-dominated trade in vegetables is the most important business of the market. Of a volume of transactions recorded totalling $259, just under 50 per cent consisted of vegetables, and just under 25 per cent consisted of European purchases of vegetables (Table VI. 6). Nearly all the vegetable trade was with the specialists. The trade in fruit, the second-ranking produce class, is similarly dominated by the Europeans on the buying side, but the sellers are rather more widely distributed. Native staple foods find few European buyers, but, when we consider the volume of this commodity brought to market, the recorded trade is surprisingly small. Even if we notionally double the trade in native staple foods, to allow for the fact that so large a proportion of villagers and New Hebridean specialists are not covered in these tables, we would still have only a total of about $60 for transactions in this group of commodities.

It is difficult to draw quantitative conclusions from Table VI. 6, especially in regard to the New Hebridean trade, since recording is so uneven. But it seems clear enough from a comparison of Table VI. 6 with earlier tables that a high proportion of goods brought to market, and especially of native staple foods brought by the villagers, remain unsold. Of foods worth $196 recorded as brought to the market on the two days in question, the most favourable estimate of sales would leave fully two-thirds unsold.

A proportion of the goods not sold at the Friday market, together

[7]Because of the close nature of the transactions, not many sales of shells by villagers to Europeans were recorded.

Table VI. 6 Percentage of the value of sales recorded in Vila market on two days of July 1965 from the survey of vendors, distinguishing class of vendor, class of produce, and ethnic group of buyers

Produce class	Europeans (%)	New Hebrideans (%)	Asians (%)	Fijians (%)	Others (%)	Total $
Sales by villagers (45 of 93 sellers)						
Native staple foods	4	28	17	13	67	14.55
Other native foods	—	—	—	—	—	—
Animal produce	33	10	21	—	—	9.10
Cooked food	3	39	1	8	33	15.40
Fruit	13	20	53	77	—	20.20
Vegetables	5	3	8	2	—	2.70
Curios	42	—	—	—	—	2.60
	100	100	100	100	100	
Total value	$6.15	$37.60	$16.30	$3.90	$0.60	$64.55
	10%	58%	25%	6%	1%	100%
Sales by New Hebridean specialists (8 of 13 sellers)						
Native staple foods	8	25	—	82	—	9.60
Other native foods	1	10	4	—	—	1.90
Animal produce	—	—	—	—	—	—
Cooked food	—	—	1	—	—	0.10
Fruit	22	20	8	9	12	8.80
Vegetables	69	45	87	9	88	31.95
Curios	—	—	—	—	—	—
	100	100	100	100	100	
Total value	$20.50	$14.20	$11.10	$5.30	$1.25	$52.35
	39%	27%	21%	10%	3%	100%
Sales by non-New Hebridean specialists (7 sellers)						
Native staple foods	6	8	—	—	—	7.20
Other native foods	1	1	4	—	—	1.00
Animal produce	2	2	—	—	—	2.40
Cooked food	—	—	—	—	—	—
Fruit	36	27	12	30	26	43.70
Vegetables	55	62	84	70	74	87·80
Curios	—	—	—	—	—	—
	100	100	100	100	100	
Total value	$87.50	$23.90	$20.00	$3.70	$7.00	$142.10
	62%	17%	14%	2%	5%	100%
Total value (all specialists)	$108.00	$38.10	$31.10	$9.00	$8.25	$194.45
	55%	20%	16%	5%	4%	100%
Total sales recorded						
Native staple foods	6	22	6	37	5	31.35
Other native foods	1	2	2	—	—	2.90
Animal produce	3	5	7	—	—	11.50
Cooked food	1	19	1	2	2	15.50
Fruit	34	23	25	36	22	72.70
Vegetables	55	29	59	25	71	122.45
Curios	2	—	—	—	—	2.60
	100	100	100	100	100	
Total value of sales	$114.15	$75.70	$47.40	$12.90	$8.85	$259.00
	44%	29%	18%	5%	4%	100%

with some new produce, is offered for sale at comparable prices at various points along the Rue Higginson on succeeding mornings. Much the most important of these off-market sites is on the steps of the Ballande store, where a sort of subsidiary market is held on other days. We recorded sales at this off-market site on two days in the week following day 3, with results summarised in Table VI. 7. Some cooked food was on sale, but fruit and vegetables formed the most important part of the goods offered; there were only very limited supplies of native staples. We do not know how many of the New Hebrideans may have been servants buying for European households. Asians, entirely Vietnamese, made almost as much use of this off-market facility as did the much more numerous European population.[8]

Table VI. 7 Value of trade recorded at off-market sites in Vila between the third and fourth market dates, by groups of vendors and ethnic groups of buyers

Sellers	Buyers				
	Europeans ($)	New Hebrideans ($)	Asians ($)	Others ($)	Total ($)
Villagers	0.30	10.78	0.30	4.20	15.58
New Hebridean specialists	4.20	4.70	2.80	—	11.70
Other specialists	8.40	12.30	5.70	—	26.40
Total	12.90	27.78	8.80	4.20	53.68

A further source of information on the habits of the buyers was provided by interviewing as many as possible of the buyers encountered in the market on the second and third market days. In this investigation some persons were interviewed more than once, and this procedure was discontinued after two weeks. Buyers were asked what they had bought and what they had paid: many went on to buy further goods after being interviewed, so Table VI. 8, which summarises the results, is in no sense complete, or comparable with Table VI. 6. There is also a strong bias in favour of English- or Pidgin-speaking informants, since only three of the interviewers, including ourselves, could put the questionnaire in French. The same general pattern of buying stands out, with its emphasis on fruit and vegetables among the Europeans, on native staples among the New Hebrideans and Fijians (with Tongans). Among the Europeans, English-speaking buyers seem to buy more

[8]We were informed by a Vietnamese vendor that Chinese buy mainly from this site, coming very early in the morning, but regret that neither we nor our assistants were present sufficiently early in the day to confirm this statement.

Table VI. 8 Value of produce, by classes, bought in Vila market by buyers of different ethnic groups interviewed on the second and third market dates, with some of the characteristics of the interviewees

Produce classes	Europeans British ($)	Europeans French ($)	New Hebrideans ($)	Vietnamese ($)	Fijians & Tongans ($)	Wallisians & Tahitians ($)	Other ($)	Total ($)
Native staple foods	4.10	0.40	15.40	—	14.60	—	3.10	37.60
Other native foods	0.50	0.90	2.60	0.20	0.50	—	0.30	5.00
Animal produce	—	—	0.50	—	3.50	—	0.50	4.50
Cooked food	0.60	—	3.30	—	—	0.10	—	4.00
Fruit	20.70	3.70	5.00	0.10	4.60	1.50	0.90	36.50
Vegetables	48.00	18.80	9.30	2.30	6.60	0.65	8.50	94.15
Curios*	2.10	—	0.40	—	0.20	—	0.20	2.90
Total purchases	76.00	23.80	36.50	2.60	30.00	2.25	13.50	184.65
No. of interviews	48	23	39	5	12	4	14	145
Total buyers interviewed	40	21	37	5	10	3	12	128
Of whom:								
Reside in Vila	39	19	29	5	10	3	11	116
Visit market at least weekly	37	17	20	3	10	2	9	98
Total of interviewees and dependants	147†	75	144	12	36	15	42	471

*Includes shells.

†Includes the largely New Hebridean crew of a British vessel.

fruit, while French-speakers buy more salad vegetables – a commentary, if scarcely a new finding, on national diet preferences.

In addition to bearing out information obtained by observing transactions from the sellers' side, the survey of buyers revealed certain basic facts about the market. Most of the buyers interviewed are regular buyers, but they represent only a small proportion of the total population. Europeans buy imported fruit and vegetables from the stores, and others use the hawkers. Few of the New Hebrideans interviewed have gardens, but both daily and weekly commuters from the villages bring food into town with them, not only for their own consumption, but also for their friends and workmates. Further, incomes are relatively high in Vila, where a labourer on the docks receives $2 per day; imported, canned, and packaged foods are within the reach of almost all the employed population and their dependants.

The viability of the market

Without doubt, most of the villagers and some of the specialists get very little return from their day at the market. The lowest value of goods brought into the market is only 10 cents, and although the highest value brought in by any one villager is $24, the highest amounts for the Fila Island and Mele villagers are both below $10 (Table VI. 9). Further, with the exception of the Fila Island women who sell almost exclusively cooked food, the villagers sell not more than about half the produce that they bring to market, and many sell less.

Of 192 sellers in the market on the first and second days together, 117 gave statements as to their gross takings for the day before leaving the market. Thereafter, we discontinued this line of inquiry to concentrate our efforts elsewhere. Among the villagers, the lowest recorded takings for the day were 20 cents, while among the specialists the lowest were $3. The highest day's takings (excluding Ho, for whom we do not present data on takings) were recorded by a specialist who stated that he had grossed $50.90, though one individual villager from Siviri in North Efaté claimed takings of $35.50.[9] If the three Siviri sellers be excluded, the highest individual gross takings recorded by a villager reached only $9.50. Some 46 of the 117 informants sold less than half the value of goods they brought to market, by their own reckoning, and very few returned from the market with all goods sold.

Cost of transport may be taken into account in assessing the net return; all sellers observed in the market for the first time on any day were asked how they had come to market, how much the journey had actually cost them, and how they would return home. Only a few

[9]It seems clear from other evidence that she was selling on behalf of companions as well as for herself.

Table VI. 9 Sundry data relating to the profitability of trading in Vila market by vendors of different groups in July 1965

	A ($)	B ($)	C* ($)	D (No.)	E ($)	F ($)
Erakor	1.00	24.00	0.20	21	1.00	9.50
Pango	0.60	7.50	0.40	25	0.20	3.60
Mele	0.60	8.60	0.80	10	1.00	6.00
Fila Island	0.10	9.15	—	32	0.50	4.00
Leleppa	2.20	15.80	2.00	11	2.90	7.00
Mosso/Siviri	3.20	13.20	6.00	11	1.50	35.50†
New Hebridean specialists	0.50	22.00	1.25‡	7	3.00	18.00
Other specialists (Ho excluded)	4.00	27.20	—	—	—	50.90§
Total recorded	0.10	27.20	—	117	0.20	50.90§

A Least value of goods brought to market by any one seller.
B Greatest value of goods brought to market by any one seller.
C Normal minimum round-trip transport cost, as stated. Exceptionally low figures are ignored.
D Number of statements of gross market income received by sellers.
E Least gross income stated by a seller.
F Greatest gross income stated by a seller.

*Including only paying-transport by taxi or bus. No allowance is made where transport is by canoe.

†Combined sales. See footnote 9 on p. 135.

‡Some walk, but this is the minimum paid by those using taxis.

§Based on a count of transactions, not on statement. Data for the non-New Hebridean specialists are too unrepresentative to be used in this way.

Note: Data for A, B, and C collected from all sellers; D, E, and F relate only to 117 sellers who stated their gross income.

specialists live within walking distance of the market, and even they use taxis if they have any quantity of goods to bring. Most Fila Islanders paddle across the harbour in their own canoes, though some use a fare-charging launch. Pango has an infrequent bus service, which is cheaper than the taxis.

In southwestern Efaté taxi fares stated were generally in keeping with the legal rates used in Table VI. 4, but where there are variations they are almost always upward. Rates are distinctly higher than the 'legal' one-way rates to North Efaté: taxis going out from Vila empty and returning loaded charge $8 from Leleppa landing, $12 from Mosso landing, and $14 from Siviri. However, almost all women coming to market, whether from near or far, share taxis, and sometimes five women and all their produce pile into one car. Individual transport costs to and from the market are thus generally less than 80 cents within the general region from Erakor and Pango to Mele, and may be as little as 30 cents, the cost of a taxi within Vila. Individual transport costs from Mosso and Leleppa lie generally around $4.40 and

$2 to $2.60 respectively. On this basis, none of the Leleppa women failed to gross more than their transport costs, but of the Mosso women only two made enough to clear the cost, while one broke even and six were, on their own showing, between $1 and $2 poorer than when they left home. The few Siviri women can cover costs only by bringing very large quantities of produce and selling them. One, who had a taxi to herself, claimed gross takings sufficient to yield her a profit of $10 over and above the round trip fare.

The marginal nature of the North Efaté share in the business, brought out in the discussion on participation in the market, is thus shown to be offset by more intensive practices, so that profit margins are as good as those achieved by many sellers living much closer to town. Some specialisation of produce, more co-operation in transport, and, at least from Siviri, co-operation in selling, enable these remote sellers – who live up to 24 miles away from the market – to compete. Intensity of organisation here produces the result that the highest net incomes recorded by any village sellers are by sellers from the remotest village.

The need for a large turnover, or for concentration on higher-value products, is apparent also much nearer to Vila, but it cannot be said to be appreciated by most village sellers from the southwestern lowland, or by some of the smaller specialists. The usual rate of pay for women in domestic service in town is $1 per day, and such work is not hard to get. Since market participation involves about two days' work, it would seem reasonable to expect a return of $2 over and above the cost of transport in order to achieve a reasonable profit by Efaté standards. But no more than about one-third of the 117 sellers for whom we have information on gross takings seem to have achieved this much.

The utility of the market to the sellers cannot, however, be measured only by their takings. A large proportion make use of a visit to Vila for purposes other than selling produce. Of 64 sellers providing information on these other activities, 25 bought fruit and vegetables in the market themselves, 23 bought cooked food, and 12 bought fish or meat. Almost none bought native staples, except for seed. More than this, however, 42 bought foodstuffs from the shops in town, and in addition to these several North Efaté women said they would remain the night in town, offer any unsold produce on the Ballande steps, and buy from the shops next morning.[10] The main food purchases in the shops were tea, sugar, rice, salt, and bread. Sixteen sellers also bought other items, particularly soap and cigarettes. For many of the women who bring

[10] This could help to reduce their transport costs, since North Efaté men working in Vila go home on Saturday and return to Vila on Sunday night. The taxi fare could be shared with these weekenders. However, few of the North Efaté women selling in the market were in fact closely related to men working in Vila.

only small quantities of goods to market, the real purpose of their participation may be to offset some of the costs of a shopping trip to town, to justify getting away for a day from house and garden duties. For these women, Vila is a metropolis and a gathering-place of friends, relatives, and interesting strangers. Bringing goods to sell in the market gives them the opportunity to enjoy these urban attractions.

The unsold native staple foods are not wasted, as the more perishable and specialised European vegetables might be. These foodstuffs are grown primarily for subsistence by villagers, and any remaining unsold can be used at home, or passed on to town-dwelling relatives and friends. We have no information about crop surplus or shortage in Erakor, Pango, Mele, or North Efaté to suggest supply variation in these villages, but garden land is generally abundant. On the occasions when we were able to question the sellers with unsold produce, some village women stated that they would give it to friends or relatives in other villages. Such practices perpetuate traditional exchange relationships between persons in different villages, and may be more appropriate to today's conditions. Fila Island has lost most of its garden land with the expansion of the town, and this is why Fila women sell mainly cooked food, providing a profit from a smaller quantity of garden produce.

We cannot estimate the cost of production for sale at the market, as for the villagers much of it is incidental to subsistence gardening. In this sense the market production is domestic surplus. However, seeds are purchased for non-native foodstuffs. A few of the specialists lease land and/or employ assistants, but the village women use only their own or family land and labour.

Vila market in perspective

The most striking feature of Vila market is its limited scale. Except by a small core, mainly specialist, it can hardly be that market participation is regarded as a financially highly profitable enterprise. For most of the vendors participation is clearly marginal, both in terms of profitability, and to their own main activities. Nor is the market of such great importance to the town, for a large proportion of the population buys very little from it, and some never go near it. Throughout this discussion, reference has been made to the retail stores which are, for a Pacific town of its size, unusually well developed in Vila. Apart from its two large and two small company stores, the town has a fair number of small Chinese general stores, and some small Vietnamese, Métis, and European-owned shops which sell food. It supports two bakeries and two butchers, the latter well supplied from nearby European plantations. As there is a very regular shipping service from Sydney, fruit and vegetables of Australian origin are readily available, though of limited range and rather high price.[11] These Vila shops sell a wide range of imported groceries, catering to French, British, Asian, and islander tastes and income levels. These include canned, frozen, and fresh fruit and vegetables which supplement or replace those sold in the market. Even among the fresh fruit and vegetables, the produce is not exactly duplicated; most are temperate-climate products such as grapes, apples, potatoes, cauliflower, and celery, and the cabbage, lettuce, tomatoes, oranges, and onions are different varieties from those sold in the market. These foods are priced by the pound or kilogram and no exact comparison with the market is possible. Because of a high wage structure, even most of the New Hebrideans employed in Vila can afford to live on a basic diet of bread, meat, and rice.

No doubt there is scope for a larger trade in locally produced fruit and vegetables, but this is unlikely to be achieved without better facilities for display and comparison, to attract more customers, and without wider adoption of retail selling practices. In the short run, at least, prospects for an expansion in the trade in native staples are very poor, unless as a result of rising prices for imported flour and rice. The trade in cooked native foods is surely capable of expansion, but it could swiftly be destroyed in its present form if some entrepreneur were to provide an outlet in the town for daily sale of these foods. The only prepared foods regularly available were baked Vietnamese sweetmeats sold from a wagon.

Even in the Pacific, Vila market is unusual. Rabaul market (Epstein 1961), which is among the largest, with a turnover of about $5,000 per week in 1961, has very large quantities of native staple foods on sale, and the same is true of the other New Guinea markets, and of urban markets at Suva and Lautoka in Fiji, Honiara in the Solomons, and Apia in Western Samoa. For its small size, Vila is a very varied market, and it neatly illustrates many aspects of intergroup relations in this ethnically diverse community. The market defies classification in the terms proposed by Bohannan and Dalton (1962: 20), since, while the villagers might in some senses be said to have only a peripheral interest in the market-place, they have a deep interest in the market economy as a whole. However, we affirm their suggestion that 'the more pervasive the market principle, the less the economic importance of the market place' (ibid: 32).

In the New Hebrides today, the most striking feature of the economy is the vigour of the two towns, Vila and Santo, well capitalised by large infusions of funds from the two metropolitan governments, and by investment of funds on the part of New Caledonian construction firms

[11]One informant claimed that the arrival of the three-weekly vessel from Australia shortly before one market day had adversely affected trade.

and other businessmen. By contrast, the European sector of the rural economy is static, except for a very few large plantations and plantation companies (Wilson 1966). With few exceptions, the 'plantations' on Efaté are in reality mixed farms, often harvesting the product of trees that it would be too costly now to replant. On Efaté many plantations derive more profit from their cattle. The native sector of the economy is expanding, though slowly and unevenly, and cash-crop methods are often very inefficient. Throughout the islands of the central part of the group, however, most people have access to a cash income, and if they wish to work on plantations, can get wages that by Pacific standards are unusually high: on Efaté $2 per day is not abnormal. Immigration into Vila and its region is substantial, especially from the small islands of the Shepherd group, but also from much further north, but though there is rapid turnover there is little prolonged unemployment, and labour shortage maintains high wages. Throughout western Efaté men can find employment if they wish, and the whole economy is to a great degree urbanised, and integrated through Vila.

There is little room for undercapitalised trading in this economy. Vila market occupies only a small and rather precarious niche in an urban supply system dominated by well-developed wholesale and retail businesses, supplying a relatively affluent population which has limited need of market-place wares. This is a situation that is not unique, though little regarded in studies of economic and social development in colonial and ex-colonial areas. Vila market is on the fringe of the urban economy of which it forms part; while it may yet recover from the catastrophic change suffered when the bulk of the Vietnamese left in 1963 it will do so mainly through more efficient production and sale of vegetables and fruit; the unspecialised, rural and traditional aspects of the market are an unprofitable anachronism.

The market of Vila plays a very small part in the local economy, and is only a main source of income for perhaps half a dozen people. For the majority of sellers the economic function is minor, and the result of a day's trading may be a loss. The market takes very little business away from the town shops, and may even bring them business, as people who make a trip to town to buy or sell in the market may spend more in the shops than normally. Efaté, and especially the native sector of its economy, is becoming increasingly involved in the market principle (Bohannan and Dalton 1962), but the place of the produce market is minor in this economic development. In the terms used by Mintz (1959) to describe the internal market systems in Haiti, Mexico, Jamaica, and Guatemala, the horizontal flow is undeveloped, as there is little specialisation among market producers which requires them to buy from one another. The New Hebridean necessities in food and manufactured imported goods are mostly purchased from shops owned by Asians or Europeans: the vertical downward flow of goods is handled outside this market. This correlates with the absence of craft work and manufactures in the New Hebrides. The market's primary flow of goods corresponds to Mintz's 'vertical upward flow', but this function is pre-empted by the specialists. As in the communities discussed by Mintz, the export (outward) flow is handled separately from the internal market. Finally, there are hardly any intermediaries in Vila.

New Hebridean villagers are involved in economic transactions more in their preparation of cash crops, especially copra, and in their wage employment on plantations and in town enterprises. All other segments of the community are fully involved in an advanced economy, and many of them came to Vila for this purpose. Vila residents, including market buyers, are mostly people who are in Vila as wage or salaried workers or entrepreneurs and depend upon town suppliers for their daily needs. For them the market is a small factor, providing Europeans with a bit of local colour, curios, dietary variety and for the islanders, supplies of the type of foods they would have in their native villages. As an institution of a small colonial town, it performs in a limited capacity, but nevertheless with a wide range of functions.

VII

Conclusion: The Market Area

H. C. Brookfield

The reader who has followed thus far through the text, taking first the introduction and then the substantive essays in turn, will certainly have recognised strong elements of similarity between the market-places discussed. When these trading places are set alongside markets studied in Africa, Asia, or middle-America, it becomes apparent that such differences as occur within the Pacific are essentially in a minor key. Such common characteristics as pricing in multiples of 10 cents, lack of bargaining, selling in village groups, absence of efforts to force a sale, short-term inflexibility of price for most classes of goods, absence of 'horizontal' trading within the market, absence of imported goods in trading – all these may be observed in market-places as widely separated in distance and cultural setting as Kerema and Apia, and point towards the conclusion that a Pacific type of market-place may be distinguished. However, this conclusion must not disregard the more commercial practices found in market-places where non-indigenous traders dominate – a caveat which the introduction sought to emphasise. But the niche occupied by the Pacific market-place in the total supply system does not depend only on cultural origins: it depends also on historical circumstances which have placed large import-export firms in a dominant position in the trade of all island groups; these circumstances are common throughout the region.

A concluding essay might seem superfluous, but we have not yet given much formal consideration to the market area, even though four of the five market studies here presented were carried out to illuminate the course of events in some part of the market area, not in the market-place itself. What I seek to do here is to examine the structure of the market area, then finally to place the Pacific market area, and the whole system, in some tentative theoretical context.

Writing of the origins of English corn markets, N.S.B. Gras (1926: 34) observed that the market area is a more significant basis for study than the market-place itself, 'for the latter is but the standing ground where events decided elsewhere take place'. This is perhaps a question of viewpoint, for the central place and its hinterland are but parts of the one system, each meaningless without the other. In the first and most influential of all theoretical discussions on the market area, von Thünen sought to explain the distribution of production around a single town in an isolated state, quite separate from the rest of the world. Though his analysis is based on data from his farm in early nineteenth-century Mecklenburg, the theoretical formulation is clearly paralleled in the Pacific market area of the late twentieth century. He found market gardening to be the activity located most closely around the town, because of the bulkiness of the product, relatively low production costs, and use of town manure: this activity thus had the highest rent of any that could be practised in the innermost ring. Immediately outward from this ring came forestry for firewood, again a product with low production costs, and with high transport costs because of its bulk, but of lower value per unit load than market garden crops and potatoes. Most of his subsequent rings were occupied by different systems of grain cultivation and grazing, because of higher production costs and lower transport costs per load, but his outermost ring of all was occupied by industrial crops. These had high production costs, were grown intensively with a high yield per unit area, but after processing and weight reduction their effective yield per unit area in terms of weight or bulk was low (Hall 1966: xxxvi-xxxix, 3-5, 195-219). In the Pacific, industrial crops and market garden crops intermingle, and at first sight the relevance of von Thünen's rings is not apparent.

It is perhaps a little more apparent if we look briefly at the much larger market systems developed to supply larger urban agglomerations in Africa, for relationships that may only tentatively be seen in the small market systems of the Pacific are there more clearly evidenced. Around the towns of the central African copper belt we find vegetables grown in an inner ring some fifty miles wide, forestry for firewood in a second ring immediately outward, and weight-reduced crops, such as tobacco, obtained from the furthest ring of all, up to eight hundred miles from the market (Miracle 1962: 316-17, Table 15). Perhaps even more striking is the market system of Tananarive, capital of Madagascar (Donque 1965-6). Here the *zoma* – the market-place – serves the needs of a city of 280,000 every day of the week, serves additionally on Fridays a surrounding rural buying area with a population of about 250,000, and has a supply area with a total population of some three millions. On Fridays there are up to 3,000 sellers and from 15,000 to 20,000 buyers in the market. The *zoma* has a continuous history of growth and diversification from its foundation some 180 years ago, and it continues to dominate the trade of the city and surrounding region, combining wholesale and retail functions, with much 'horizontal' trade within the market, some goods being sold for resale in other parts of the country. Even in the city the shops have acquired only a small and specialised part of the trading system.[1]

Rings may clearly be distinguished in the supply area of the Tananarive system. An innermost ring, partly within the city area, specialises in intensive vegetable production, while in a second ring a few miles out less intensive vegetable production mingles with the intensive production of rice. Both inner rings were supplied with manure from the town. A third ring is the main producing area of rice and root crops, and extends about sixty miles from the market-place. Beyond this is a fourth ring within which there are a number of other market towns, each with its own inner supplying rings, but from which some production, even of vegetables and fruit, travels to Tananarive. Some of these small market-places of the fourth ring serve as relay markets in an hierarchical relationship to Tananarive; cattle and some non-perishable goods pass through a chain of these relay markets before reaching the capital. Finally, there is even a fifth ring, including most of the western and south-central parts of Madagascar, whence cattle and products of the tropical lowlands are sent to the Tananarive *zoma*.

The largest of Pacific towns is less than one-fifth the size of Tananarive, and all large towns are well supplied with company stores and other retail businesses; the scale of the market-place business is very much smaller and more ill-developed. This being so, the market areas are often quite surprisingly extensive. Apia is supplied from most parts of the island of Upolu and even receives a little from Savai'i; Honiara gets regular supplies from Aola, forty-five miles down the coast; Vila receives produce from places up to twenty-six miles distant; and Suva, Nouméa, and Papeete are all supplied from much further afield. Koki

[1]A French chain-store company that is the most vigorous competitor of the market-place in the sale of food and small goods has an operation of much more limited size in Tananarive than in Nouméa, even though the European and Europeanised population of Tananarive is alone larger than the whole population of Nouméa. This dominance of the market-place is a very general feature in central Malagasy towns, and is even more evident in smaller places such as Betafo, Ambatolampy, and even Antsirabe with its important expatriate element; in each of these towns the few shops merely stand around the edges of the market-place where the bulk of trading is carried on.

market at Port Moresby receives some supplies by air from the other side of New Guinea. Among large market-places in the Pacific area, perhaps only Rabaul has a closely confined market area, very little coming from more than sixteen miles away. Given more data, it might be possible to obtain some functional relationship between the scale of market-place trading, the density of population in the environs, and the extent of the market area; there is evidence to suggest that such a relationship exists.

Zonation in the market area

In examining the question of zonation within Pacific market areas it is first essential to note that in the absence of horizontal trading the supply area of the market is almost always far wider than the buying area; with few exceptions the latter is confined to the towns themselves. The cane-farmers of the Fiji sugar belt are a partial exception, and wherever there is a fish market rural populations may come to buy from a wide area; this is most strikingly seen at Papeete, where most of the animal protein consumed in the whole island of Tahiti is in the form of fish bought in the *marché central* (Anderson 1963: 103-5). Some planters or their agents also visit urban markets to buy food for their workers, and pursers of ships in harbour may obtain food for their crews. A few residents of the mining town of Forari, forty miles east, buy in Vila market. In the main, however, it is the urban populations themselves that buy the overwhelming bulk of produce offered, and the nature of their demand curves for produce in the market-place is greatly affected by the elasticity of substitution between market-place foodstuffs and shop-bought imported goods. Also there is a number of gardens within the urban area of many Pacific towns, which are not closely-built. Some of the production of these gardens is sold around the town by hawkers, much is consumed by the growers themselves and their associates, and only a part is put on sale in the market-place. The effect of these urban gardens may, in fact, be to restrict demand rather than to increase supply in the market.

The evidence of zonation in the supply area is not easy to interpret. The bi-weekly market at Honiara is supplied mainly from the two villages closest to the town, the bi-monthly market from further out. Within Tasimboko West there seems to be a gradation between places close to Honiara which supply more perishable vegetables, and those further away which supply mainly native staple foods. At Vila the bulk of the perishable European vegetables are supplied by the specialists, most of whom live and garden within five miles of the town. At Apia very little produce indeed comes into the market from the inner-urban fringe, but 58 per cent of the supply of vegetables comes from the crowded villages of northwestern Upolu, from two to ten miles west of Apia, while 82 per cent of the bulky root crops are drawn from a zone between one and thirty-eight miles out, mostly from places beyond the innermost villages. At Suva a zone of market gardens, worked mainly but not exclusively by Indians, surrounds the city to north and north-east, and supplies most of the perishables and non-perishables alike. However, production is more intensive and holdings are smaller towards the city than further away (Nandan 1957: 37-8). There is a similar situation around Nouméa, where most of the risky, perishable crops requiring watering and intensive care are grown immediately around and even within the city, or else at La Foa, seventy-three miles away (Saussol 1967: 49). Non-perishables and all less-demanding crops reach Nouméa from a much wider area, including even the Loyalty Islands (Tonnelier *et al.* 1966).

Perhaps we may tentatively suggest that there are three potential zones or rings[2] in Pacific market areas, but that in any individual case up to two of these may be absent. The inner ring is generally of distorted shape where recognisable, and characterised by the presence of specialist gardeners who put much of their effort into profitable but risky lines, especially European and Chinese fresh vegetables. Some of this production reaches consumers through hawkers, or through shops and institutions under regular arrangements, but much passes through the market-place. The existence of the first ring generally requires the presence of a class of persons, usually with limited land, often rented, sometimes cultivated with employed labour, sometimes only a part-time activity. Some villagers may participate in this specialised production, but most participants are non-locals – often Asian, sometimes European – and if indigenous, generally living away from their home areas. Sellers from this ring are often men, whereas women dominate from the outer rings.

This first ring, where it occurs, is generally an intrusion into the space of a second, a 'main supplying ring', of width depending largely on the size of the market and on the availability and cost of transport. This is *par excellence* the domain of the village producer-seller, though in some market areas specialised middlemen may buy the produce at the market for resale from licensed stalls. Type of production, efficiency of operation, and degree of dependence on the market as a source of income are all highly variable throughout this ring. Other things being equal – which they seldom if ever are – we tend to find a diminution in the proportion of risky fresh vegetables offered as we go outward from

[2]The terms 'zone' and 'ring' are used for simplicity, and because they are current in the literature. In fact the shape of these rings is elongated along transport routes, narrowed between them, so that the actual pattern is more likely to resemble a star, often truncated on one side by the sea.

the market-place, and an increase in the proportion of goods with a high value in proportion to bulk, combined with low perishability. The more unreliable and scarce the means of transport, the more likely we are to find this gradient, which is illustrated well in Tasimboko West. By contrast it is absent around Apia, where good bus services operate cheaply throughout Upolu. The basic offering of this ring is the native staple foods, sold to urban natives in the market-place, with a proportion traded outside the market-place by daily or weekly commuters from the producing villages who work in town, or given to men working in the town by women who come to sell in the market and also for other purposes.

In every market area where this main supplying ring is well developed some villages participate much more in the market than others, and participation also varies from time to time in accordance with cash needs. A complex of factors enters into this situation, including presence or absence or alternative sources of cash income, availability of land for annual crops, the state of the market for perennial cash crops, and especially the presence or absence of a few individuals within a village who have decided to utilise the market-place as a main source of cash income in preference to other means. For the villagers, decisions on whether or not to use the market-place, and if so how and when to use it, depend on a further complex of considerations. These include their interest in going periodically to town, and their preference for cultivating annual or field crops rather than perennial cash crops – which in turn is affected by the nature and size of their land holdings and rights, their preferences as between wage and agricultural labour and other entrepreneurial activities, their need for frequent if small supplies of ready cash, their willingness and ability to accept and adapt their production and activities to the risks of the market-place and especially to the risks of transport to the market-place, and their trading-partner relationships with particular market customers, middlemen, carriers or *colporteurs*. There is probably only a minority of individuals in any village with the ability skilfully to use the opportunities of the market-place with sustained success. Always there is a large number of villagers, often a majority, who see in the market-place only an opportunity to pick up occasional spot cash, or to defray costs of visits to town which they undertake without much planning, or who simply take along a few roots, greens, or other goods as a kind of gamble when going to town, simply for the fun of it, not being unduly worried if they fail to make a sale.

But despite this wide freedom of choice within the main supplying ring, its outer limits are fairly precisely drawn by economic considerations. Often the limit is quite abrupt, at the end of a road system, the beach where the sea journey comes to an end, the edge of the uncleared forest. Beyond the end of a road system or inland from the beach, human porterage becomes necessary and the quantities that can be carried fall at once, along with the willingness to carry them. Even so, there is some participation at Honiara from the Paripao bush, at Rabaul occasionally from the Bainings, at Santo from the Middle Bush. Where there are no such sharp limits, as in North Efaté or eastern Upolu, or along the coast of Guadalcanal, the limits are drawn by mounting transport costs, coupled with increasing difficulty in obtaining transport. Often all available transport is based in the market town, and in any case all fuel has to be obtained there; rates may steepen with distance. Participation in the market may continue to be profitable, but only by selecting items of high value in proportion to bulk and low perishability, or by bringing a quantity of goods to market sufficient to pay the cost of transport. It is this necessary increase in scale that finally determines the limit for the producer-seller.

If the roads go on, or if the sea is used for transport to market, we have a third ring, the domain of the *colporteur.*[3] Beyond the economic limit of the main supplying ring is a wide zone in which only the large and specialised grower with his own transport can afford regularly to dispense with the *colporteur.* The latter will fix his buying price as closely as possible to production costs, or to the minimum price which the grower will accept as worth the effort of producing the crops; by bearing the whole risk of resale, he then has a good chance of profit. The width of this zone in Fiji, and especially in New Caledonia – where the main supplying ring has few suppliers – is remarkable, but no less so than in French Polynesia, where the government, acting as *colporteur*, can report a profit on a sea haul of 350 miles. In a territory with several markets, such as Fiji, this third ring is common to a number of market areas, and its existence there helps to reduce price differentials which exist between the different market-places. The inner ring of the specialists and the outer ring of the *colporteurs* are the most 'commercial' and least 'traditional' parts of the market area in mode of operation: it is thus in market areas where both are well developed that we should expect to find commercial practices most strongly developed.

[3]In the Sigatoka valley in Fiji (see Map 9), Spate notes that the lower valley supplies the small market at Sigatoka by producer-sellers, while the upper valley sends goods mainly to the sugar belt markets (where prices are higher than in Suva) by *colporteur.* He attributes this to the fact that only the lower valley people can get to Sigatoka in time to sell in this small-demand market-place: *colporteurs* could certainly do so, and some do, but prospects of a sale are better elsewhere. This seems to be a case of a small market area existing within the outer ring of a larger market area or areas (Spate 1959:49).

Some wider considerations of the market area

Especially the width of this outer ring, but also the range of freedom of choice within the main supplying ring, both reveal a basic characteristic of the market area in the Pacific, namely the size of the margin between production costs and selling prices in the market-place. For the village producer, and the specialist who grows most of his own basic food requirements without employing labour, production costs can be measured only in terms of land and time that could otherwise be used for other purposes: that is, the basis of cost determination must be comparative rather than absolute, and the minimum acceptable level of returns is in part governed by returns available from other activities. Similarly, the selling prices must be evaluated in terms of the satisfactions that money can supply. In the present early stage of research on work organisation among Pacific societies, or on family budgets in these same areas, it is impossible to express these equations in quantitative terms, but a few general points may be made.

Where market crops are identical with subsistence crops, or can be produced by similar techniques in the same sort of garden, a small amount of market production can be undertaken with only a marginal addition to family work schedules, and the principal time input is in fact in the preparation of crops for market and in the marketing process itself. Since the journey is often made from choice rather than necessity, the actual production cost is very small indeed. The man who goes in more seriously for market gardening has to use time and land that he might otherwise employ for perennial cash crops, and his crops demand more frequent land preparation and planting than perennial crops, though much less time in harvesting and preparation for market.

Carriage is a more serious question. Except with cooked foods, there is no significant loss of weight between the crop as harvested and as marketed. This is in contrast to the alternative perennial cash crops, such as copra, cocoa, and coffee: with all these crops there is a weight loss of between 70 and 85 per cent between the crop as harvested and the final saleable product. Thus in weighing up the alternative of selling whole coconuts in the market or of making copra, the producer has to consider not only the potential difference in cash returns, and the amount of time involved, but also the fact that he has to transport to market a load of bulky and heavy nuts that would make only a few pounds weight of saleable produce if converted into copra. The considerations that apply to decisions between growing field crops for sale in the market, or perennial crops for sale to traders after processing, are less direct but none the less similar.

Further, many of the market-place cash crops are exacting in terms of the time when they must be marketed. They cannot be stored for long, or left in the ground or on the tree for harvesting and processing at a convenient time; if not harvested and sold at the right time the crop is altogether lost. This consideration applies especially to the grower of European or Chinese vegetables and fruit. The discipline of specialised market gardening may thus require the grower frequently to forego other satisfactions, such as participation in some local event. Specialised market gardeners growing fresh vegetables are thus to be found nearest the town, where returns are most immediate and urban satisfactions most readily obtained, or else among more distant men with a particularly strong profit motive, such as Lasaqa's Samuel Saki at Koli in Tasimboko, or the part-Seychellese on the plateau above Mele in Efaté.

Not many market-garden producers depend wholly on the one business; even in New Caledonia most farms at La Foa are mixed, with livestock and coffee as secondary enterprises. But where farmers do depend mainly on market gardening, as northeast of Suva in Fiji, the return for fairly hard work is good. Ward showed that a gross return of $225 per acre was normal from market-garden crops, and that with more intensive methods taro could return $450 per acre, pineapples even without fertiliser as much as $675, and *yaqona* (kava) even more (Ward 1965: 182). By contrast gross returns from copra are more variable; with a normal yield of about 4 cwt per acre and a price of $100 per ton, gross returns would reach only $20 per acre. Under good conditions bananas as a cash crop for export could yield incomes over $180 per acre, but seldom produce anything like this (Ward 1965: 203).

Given comparisons of this sort, it is not difficult to see how such high transport costs – either borne directly or through *colportage* – can be accepted by producers quite far from the market-place. Indeed, entrepreneurship in the carrying business or *colportage* is probably the only significantly more profitable channel of activity open to villagers, and this requires much more specialised knowledge, and capital for transport. The stable and relatively high price structure of Pacific market-places is sustained by high town incomes of which only a small part is spent on food, and by the 'collective bargaining' of the sellers: as a result market gardening is a business in which profits may be made at small real cost over a wide area. The more developed and differentiated the economy, the larger is the buying area, and the wider the spread of profit opportunities. Finney's elder Tahitian was expressing his satisfaction at this state of affairs when he declared Tahiti a paradise because he could throw his net in the lagoon a few times, and promptly sell the fish for wine to women returning from work in the factory (Finney 1965a: 325-6). The essence of the wide spreading of profit is the large number of producers, each offering only a limited quantity of goods and hence not requiring to make a large outlay of

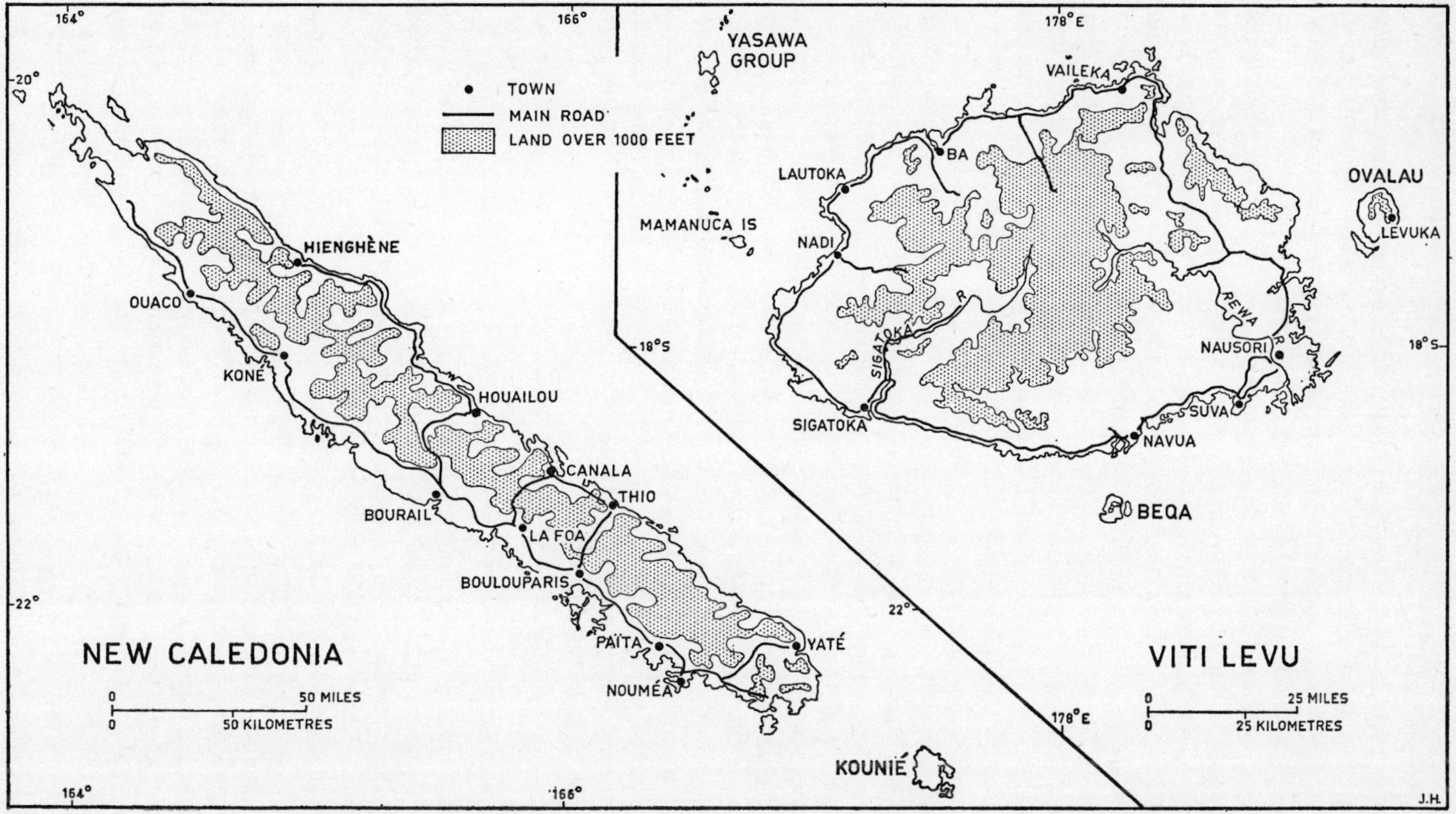

Map 9 *New Caledonia and Viti Levu, Fiji, showing towns mentioned in the text, and roads*

effort in order to do so. Specialists, middlemen, carriers, and *colporteurs* are in smaller number, and the latter groups especially are able to make a very handsome return on their investment as a result of shortage of the necessary means of transport.

By means of this high relative profitability of market participation, town and country are integrated over quite wide areas, and people are able to travel into town for a variety of purposes more frequently, to the benefit of all sorts of urban enterprises. Returning rural dwellers can bring back supplies for village trade stores, thus increasing the motive for specialisation in the rural areas. But the wide spread, and the low level of individual incomes obtained from a business of limited total scale, go hand in hand. It is only the rapid growth of the towns which creates opportunities for specialist market gardeners to enter the business, and for new villagers to participate as roads are improved and extended, without destroying the profit margin of those already in the business.[4] With growing capital accumulation and interest in entrepreneurship this is a situation which can hardly continue indefinitely, and there seems little reason to doubt that favourably located entrepreneurs could, by expanding their own production and breaching the solid front of price maintenance, crowd the poorly-placed sellers out of the market, and in so doing also reduce the share of imported goods in the whole system of supply. Rational planning, which should include transport improvements, regulation of *colportage*, and action to restrict competing imports of overseas produce, seems to be necessary if the impetus in creating urbanised regions out of the present market areas is to be sustained.

Conclusion: some theoretical considerations of the market system

If producers in Pacific market areas were to specialise in the form of production which would yield them the highest rent, it seems probable that a separation into something very like von Thünen's rings would occur. However, the markets are supplied mainly by non-specialists, most of whom have other cash-producing alternatives, and in addition the web of interpersonal support provided within the traditional economy. The specialist participants – market gardeners, carriers, and *colporteurs* – are mainly instrumental in creating the measure of zonation that exists, whether by their own productive and trading activities, or through their provision of transportation; a high proportion of these people are non-indigenes, or at least are not indigenous to the areas in which they operate. In this situation, a model which assumes the profit maximisation motive is inadequate, and we would do better to

[4]It is possible that this was happening at Vila in 1965. New specialists were entering the market-place, and village selling was strikingly unsuccessful.

proceed by examining the choices open to the individual inhabitant of the market area, and to consider how these choices are influenced by distance from the market. This is more than the need simply to consider the manner in which farmers—satisficers rather than maximisers—deviate in their choice of land use from the rigid solutions of agricultural location theory. Pred (1967: 67-8) succinctly reviews the considerations that a Thünenian farmer would have to bear in mind:

> the farmer would, among other things, have to: determine transport costs and rates per unit of farm area to all possible market-outlet permutations on all production-alternative permutations at every imaginable scale and intensity: compute labor and capital inputs per unit of land on all possible production-alternative permutations at every imaginable scale and intensity (a task complicated by the fact that the cost of labor and capital inputs will themselves tend to be a function of the farm's distance from various market centers); be fully aware of all relevant local, regional and/or national relationships between the supply and demand of every production alternative . . . know the yields obtainable from all present soil types . . . possess perfect climatic foresight . . . On top of all this, the farmer somehow would have to resolve the usually irresolvable conflict between seeking short-run and long-run maximum returns.

The Pacific farmer, in addition, would need to predict the incidence upon him of obligations within the traditional system of reciprocal aid and the possibilities of obtaining such aid when he is himself in need, and be able accurately to measure the relative satisfactions obtainable from time-scheduled market production, cash-crop production of kinds that can be taken up or put down at will, leisure and the opportunity to participate at will in the affairs of the local community. In all this he needs not only to be a cost/benefit analyst of his own activities in relation to competing neighbours, but also to co-ordinate his own enterprises with those of neighbours with whom he collaborates in a wide range of activities, and with those of the 'field' of persons with whom he is in a relationship of reciprocal aid.

It is apparent that the majority of Pacific farmers meet this uncertainty situation by producing a 'normal surplus', in Allan's (1965: 38-48) sense; the existence of such a surplus in the Pacific region has now been demonstrated by a number of workers, from New Guinea to Samoa. At the same time they arm themselves with a range of choices for cash-acquisition, having among other things both a marketable surplus of foodstuffs and a planting of long-term cash crops that may be tapped at will. They may also sell their labour, invest individually or with others in some enterprise, acquire and disburse cash and other benefits through the system of reciprocal aid. They may also gamble. Faced with a range of choices which they are not equipped to evaluate relatively to one another, they distribute their activities among the alternatives. Certainly they are satisficers rather than maximisers, but more than this they are multiple-insurers who diffuse their inputs through a wide range of enterprises, thus seeming to place more emphasis on the minimisation of risk than on the maximisation of profit. A diffused distribution of land uses results, but the fact that some weak zonation does emerge reveals that they are able in rough terms to assess and balance the relative risk and relative profitability of those enterprises which show variation in these respects with distance from the market-place.

In the same way, it is not adequate to interpret the activity of the market-place itself in terms only of the theory of demand and supply. Substitution of shop-purchases on the part of buyers, and of alternative activities on the part of sellers, combine with physical limitations to the short-term elasticity of demand and supply and cause both sets of curves to show both inflexion and inversion. As a result the curves often intersect at a wide angle, yet small changes in demand or supply do not cause the wide swings in price that theory would demand in these circumstances. In the typical Pacific market-place these swings do not occur because of conservative price policies, and because most sellers are not concerned primarily with the maximisation of profit. The point of this argument is reinforced by the exceptional situation at Nouméa (Angleviel 1961), where wide price swings do occur and the result has been periods of chaos throughout the system, leading to a demand for price stability.

All this is not to say that our normal tools for the understanding of price formation and of the location of activities do not have their place. They suggest forces which operate on the market system to restrict the freedom of choice, and to influence choice within these limits. Furthermore, some elements of the market system are more sensitive to these forces than are others. In general we may say that the producer with a great risk-bearing element in market participation is more highly influenced by considerations formalised in maximiser theories, such as the theories of price and agricultural location, than is the market producer who has varied additional sources of income. It is clear then that in understanding these market systems we must take account of their social and behavioural setting as much as of their economic and regional setting. While this collection of essays certainly does not attain such a full comprehension, it may at least provide some augmentation of our means for analysing the *modus operandi* of trading systems in the Pacific, and perhaps also in other developing regions of the world.

Bibliography

Allan, W. (1965). *The African husbandman.* Edinburgh (Oliver and Boyd).

Anderson, E. (1963). 'Tahitian bonito fishing'. *Kroeber Anthropological Society Papers* **28**:87-120.

Angleviel, J. (1961). 'Les problèmes du maraîchage en Nouvelle-Calédonie'. *Revue du centre de productivité et d'études économiques* **1**:22-37.

Bauer, P. T. (1954). *West African trade: a study of competition, oligopoly and monopoly in a changing economy.* Cambridge (Cambridge University Press).

Beaver, W. N. (1920). *Unexplored New Guinea: a record of the travels, adventures and experiences of a resident magistrate amongst the head-hunting savages and cannibals of the unexplored interior of New Guinea.* London (Seeley, Service).

Belshaw, C. S. (1964). *Under the Ivi tree: society and economic growth in rural Fiji.* London and Berkeley (Routledge and Kegan Paul, University of California Press).

—— (1965). *Traditional exchange and modern markets.* Englewood Cliffs, N. J. (Prentice Hall).

Bohannan, P. and Dalton, G. (1962). *Markets in Africa: eight subsistence economies in transition.* Evanston, Ill. (Northwestern University Press).

Brookfield, H. C. and Brown, Paula (1963). *Struggle for land: agriculture and group territories among the Chimbu of the New Guinea highlands.* Melbourne (Oxford University Press).

BSIP (British Solomon Islands Protectorate) (1951-). *Department of Agriculture Annual Reports.* Honiara (Government Printer).

—— (1957). *Third quarterly report of the Agricultural Field Officer, Central Solomons.* Honiara (Government Printer).

—— (1959). Department of Labour Annual Report (typescript). Honiara.

—— (1964). *Report of the Agricultural Officer, Central Solomons (January-June).* Honiara (Government Printer).

—— (1966). *Roads Policy.* White Paper No. 9. Honiara (Government Printer).

Bulmer, R. N. H. (1962). 'Chimbu plume traders'. *Australian Natural History* **14**:15-19.

Burns, A., Watson, T. Y., and Peacock, A. T. (1960). *Report of the Commission of Enquiry into the natural resources and population trends of the colony of Fiji.* Legislative Council of Fiji, Council Paper No. 1. Suva (Government Printer).

Burton, J. W. (1910). *The Fiji of today.* London (Kelly).

Commonwealth of Australia (1924-5, 1927-8). *Annual Reports on the Territory of New Guinea.* Canberra (Government Printer).

Couper, A. D. (1967). The island trade: an analysis of the environment and operation of seaborne trade among three island groups in the Pacific. Ph.D. thesis, Australian National University.

Crocombe, R. G. (1964). *Land tenure in the Cook Islands.* Melbourne (Oxford University Press).

Dakeyne, R. B. (1965). Stability and change in the Yega economy. M.A. thesis, University of Sydney.

Dalton, G. (1965). 'Primitive, archaic and modern economies: Karl Polanyi's contribution to economic anthropology and comparative economy'. In June Helm (ed.), *Essays in economic anthropology dedicated to the memory of Karl L. Polanyi.* Proceedings of the 1965 Annual Spring Meeting of the American Ethnological Society (Seattle).

—— (in press). 'Theoretical issues in economic anthropology'. *Current Anthropology.*

Davidson, J. W. (1967). *Samoa mo Samoa: the emergence of the independent state of Western Samoa.* Melbourne (Oxford University Press).

Demene, F. (1962). 'Sur le maraîchage'. *Revue du centre de productivité et d'études économiques* **3**:22-37.

Dewey, Alice (1962). *Peasant marketing in Java.* New York (Free Press of Glencoe).

Donque, G. (1965-6). 'Le Zoma de Tananarive: étude géographique d'un marché urbain'. *Madagascar Revue de Géographie* **7**:93-227; **8**:93-245.

Doumenge, F. (1966). *L'homme dans le Pacifique Sud: étude géographique.* Publications de la Société des Océanistes No. 19. Paris (Musée de l'Homme).

Dubbledam, L. F. B. (1964). 'The devaluation of the Kapauku-cowrie as a factor of social disintegration'. *American Anthropologist* **66**, 2(4), Special Publication, New Guinea, the central highlands: 293-303.

Epstein, T. Scarlett (1961). 'A study of Rabaul market'. *Australian Journal of Agricultural Economics* **5**:1-18.

—— (1968). *Capitalism, primitive and modern.* Canberra (Australian National University Press).

Finney, B. R. (1965a). 'Polynesian peasants and proletarians: socio-economic change among the Tahitians of French Polynesia'. *Journal of the Polynesian Society* **74**:269-328.

—— (1965b). 'Economic change and dietary consequences among the Tahitians'. *Micronesia* **2**:1-14.

Firth, R. (1939). *Primitive Polynesian economy.* London (Routledge).

Fuchs, L. H. (1961). *Hawaii pono: a social history.* New York (Harcourt, Brace and World).

Germany, Government of (1910-11). German New Guinea Annual Reports (translated from the German by H. A. Thomson) (typescript). Canberra, National Library of Australia.

Gras, N. S. B. (1926). *Evolution of the English corn market from the twelfth to the eighteenth century.* Cambridge, Mass. (Harvard University Press).

Groves, M. C. (1960). 'Motu pottery'. *Journal of the Polynesian Society* **69**:3-22.

Guiart, J. (1963). *Structure de la chefferie en Melanésie du Sud.* Université de Paris, Travaux et mémoires de l'Institut d'Ethnologie No. 66. Paris (Institut d'Ethnologie, Hachette).

Hall, P. G. (ed.) (1966). *Von Thünen's Isolated State: an English edition of Der isolierte Staat* (translated by Carla M. Wartenberg). Oxford (Pergamon Press).

Harding, T. G. (1967). *Voyagers of the Vitiaz Strait: a study of a New Guinea trade system.* Seattle and London (University of Washington Press).

Hogbin, G. R. (1964). *A survey of indigenous rubber producers in the Kerema Bay area.* New Guinea Research Bulletin No. 5. Canberra.

Hogbin, H. I. (1939). *Experiments in civilization: the effects of European culture on a native community of the Solomon Islands.* London (Routledge).

——(1947). 'Native trade around the Huon Gulf, northeastern New Guinea'. *Journal of The Polynesian Society* **56**:242-55.

Howlett, Diana R. (1962). A decade of change in the Goroka valley, New Guinea: land use and development in the 1950s. Ph.D. thesis, Australian National University.

Iskandar, A. (1964). *Irian Barat: pembangunan suku Mukoko.* Sukarnapura (Universitas Tjenderawasih).

Leahy, M. (1930-4). Diaries for 1930-34 (MS.). Canberra, National Library of Australia.

Le Borgne, J. (1964). *Géographie de la Nouvelle-Calédonie et des îles Loyauté.* Nouméa (Ministère de l'Education, de la Jeunesse et des Sports).

Leenhardt, M. (1937). *Gens de la Grande Terre: (Nouvelle-Calédonie).* Paris (Gallimard).

Malinowski, B. (1915). 'The natives of Mailu'. *Transactions and Proceedings of the Royal Society of South Australia* **34**:494-706.

——(1922). *Argonauts of the western Pacific.* London (Routledge).

McCarthy, J. K. (1963). *Patrol into yesterday: my New Guinea years.* Melbourne (Cheshire).

McTaggart, W. D. (1963). Nouméa: a study in social geography. Ph.D. thesis, Australian National University.

Meggitt, M. J. (1958). 'The Enga of the New Guinea highlands: some preliminary observations'. *Oceania* **28**:253-330.

Mintz, S. W. (1959). 'Internal market systems as mechanisms of social articulation'. In V. Ray (ed.), *Intermediate societies, social mobility and communication.* Proceedings of the 1959 Annual Spring Meeting of the American Ethnological Society: 20-30. Seattle.

Miracle, M. P. (1962). 'African markets and trade in the Copperbelt'. In P. Bohannan and G. Dalton, *African markets.* Evanston, Ill. (Northwestern University Press).

Nandan, S. (1957). 'Market gardening on the Suva peninsula'. *Agricultural Journal (Fiji)* **28**:37-9.

NID (Naval Intelligence Division, United Kingdom Admiralty) (1945). *Geographical Handbook Series, Pacific Islands, I. General Survey.* London (Naval Intelligence Division).

Nilles, J. (1944). 'Natives of the Bismarck Mountains, New Guinea, II'. *Oceania* **15**:1-18.

——(1950). 'The Kuman of the Chimbu region, central highlands, New Guinea'. *Oceania* **21**:25-65.

Pisier, G. (1962). *Esquisse d'un plan de développement économique et social de la Nouvelle-Calédonie.* Nouméa (Haut Commissariat de la France dans le Pacifique, Bureau du Commerce Extérieur).

Platt, B. S. (1945). *Tables of representative values of foods commonly used in tropical countries.* Medical Research Council, Special Report Series No. 253. London (H.M.S.O.).

Polanyi, K. (1957). 'The economy as instituted process'. In K. Polanyi, C. M. Arensberg, and H. W. Pearson (eds.), *Trade and market in the early empires: economies in history and theory:* 243-79. New York (Free Press of Glencoe).

Pospisil, L. (1958). *Kapauku Papuans and their law.* Yale University Publications in Anthropology No. 54. (New Haven, Yale).

——(1963). *Kapauku Papuan economy.* Yale University Publications in Anthropology No. 67. (New Haven, Yale).

Pred, A. (1967). Behavior and location: foundations for a geographic and dynamic location theory, Part I. *Lund Studies in Geography.* Ser. B, Human Geography No. 27.

Reay, Marie (1959). *The Kuma: freedom and conformity in the New Guinea highlands.* Melbourne (Melbourne University Press).

Reilly, W. J. (1929). *Methods for the study of retail relationships.* Bureau of Business Research, Research Monograph No. 4. Austin (University of Texas). (Reprinted 1959.)

Sahlins, M. D. (1962). *Moala: culture and nature on a Fijian island.* Ann Arbor (University of Michigan Press).

——(1965). 'Exchange-value and the diplomacy of primitive trade'. In June Helm (ed.), *Essays in economic anthropology, dedicated to the memory of Karl L. Polanyi.* Proceedings of the 1965 Annual Spring Meeting of the American Ethnological Society. Seattle.

Saussol, A. (1967). 'La Foa agricultural settlement in New Caledonia'. *South Pacific Bulletin* **17**:47-50.

Sautot, H. (1949). *Grandeur et décadence du Gaullisme dans le Pacifique.* Melbourne (Cheshire).

Seligman, C. G. (1910). *The Melanesians of British New Guinea.* Cambridge (Cambridge University Press).

Singh Uberoi, J. P. (1962). *Politics of the Kula ring.* Manchester (Manchester University Press).

Spate, O. H. K. (1959). *The Fijian people: economic problems and prospects.* Legislative Council of Fiji, Council Paper No. 13. Suva (Government Printer).

Thompson, Laura (1940). *Southern Lau, Fiji: an ethnography.* Bernice P. Bishop Museum Bulletin No. 162, Honolulu.

Tonnelier, A. *et al.* (1966). 'Enquête sur le marché de consommation de Nouméa en légumes et fruits de production locale'. *Perspectives Calédoniennes* (La Jeune Chambre Economique de la Nouvelle-Calédonie) **2**:9-28.

Veldkamp, F. (1958). Nota over de Baliem-vallei van Controleur F. Veldkamp (MS.). Hollandia.

Ward, R. G. (1965). *Land use and population in Fiji: a geographical study.* Great Britain, Department of Technical Co-operation, Overseas Research Publication No. 9, London (H.M.S.O.).

Williams, F. E. (1932). 'Trading voyages from the Gulf of Papua'. *Oceania* **3**:139-66.

——(1940). *Drama of Orokolo: the social and ceremonial life of the Elema.* Oxford (Clarendon Press).

Wilson, J. S. G. (1966). *An economic survey of the New Hebrides.* Great Britain, Ministry of Overseas Development, Overseas Research Publication No. 15. London (H.M.S.O.).

WPHC (Western Pacific High Commission) (1963). *The laws of the British Solomon Islands Protectorate.* Honiara (Government Printer).

Zipf, G. K. (1949). *Human behaviour and the principle of least effort: an introduction to human ecology.* Cambridge, Mass. (Addison Wesley Press).

Index

Text set in 10/12 point Linotype Monticello, a type modelled on an early American face and first used in a fifty-volume collection of the *Papers of Thomas Jefferson*.

Printed on 85gsm Burnie University Text by The Specialty Press Limited, North Clayton, Victoria.